### The

We have this hero-rescue i
We *can't* fail because wh
dies. It's very hard for us to accept the fact that there are
things that are out of our control. . . .

### The Fear

We heard there was a major highway pileup, and the
closer we got, the worse it sounded. Someone said a hundred cars were involved. There were people with multiple
injuries. I kept thinking, "God, I wish I had a parachute.
I'd jump right out of this bird. . . ."

### The Doubts

The kid was dying and the administrative part of the hospital didn't give a damn. We had to make a decision fast.
We gave the kid two units of blood and loaded her on the
helicopter for a flight to another part of the state. They
took her right in as soon as we got there. She was in the
hospital three weeks, but she fully recovered. . . .

### The Danger

During one night flight, visibility outside was so bad the
pilot needed a darkened interior so he could attempt to see
the ridge lines of the mountains up ahead. So he turned
our cabin lights off. Our patient was hanging in there, but
there was little I could do medically under those conditions. If we all went down, it wouldn't make any difference what I had done. . . .

### *From* Flight for Life

---

**Books by Marie Bartlett Maher**

Flight for Life
Trooper Down

Published by POCKET BOOKS

# FLIGHT FOR LIFE

## MARIE BARTLETT MAHER

POCKET BOOKS

New York   London   Toronto   Sydney   Tokyo   Singapore

An *Original* Publication of POCKET BOOKS

POCKET BOOKS, a division of Simon & Schuster Inc.
1230 Avenue of the Americas, New York, NY 10020

ISBN: 0-671-74464-X

First Pocket Books printing May 1993

10  9  8  7  6  5  4  3  2  1

POCKET and colophon are registered trademarks
of Simon & Schuster Inc.

Cover photo by Faustino Sirven/The Image Bank

Printed in the U.S.A.

*To uncle Bill,*
*who enriched my past.*

*And to my husband, Mike Maher,*
*who enriches both the present and the future.*

# ACKNOWLEDGMENTS

Writing an acknowledgment for a book is like giving an acceptance speech at the Academy Awards. There are always more people to thank than time and audience interest allow, and there is always the fear that someone or something will not be mentioned.

So it is with some trepidation that I set out to express my thanks to those who helped me secure and complete this project. And writing a book *is* a project—a major undertaking that involves not only huge amounts of time and commitment, but full cooperation from the people about whom the book is written.

Therefore, my first debt of gratitude goes to the flight nurses, paramedics, pilots, and other medical personnel throughout the states I visited, who willingly, cheerfully, allowed me access to both their private and professional worlds. A special thanks to Greg Lathrop, chief flight nurse at Memorial Mission Hospital in Asheville, North Carolina, and his entire crew, who not only bore my frequent visits and countless questions with good humor, but managed to squeeze me into their helicopter for a memorable ride or two. The team also provided me with coffee, chitchat, and background information on medical flight programs, all of which proved invaluable.

## Acknowledgments

A great deal of credit for the book goes to my editor, Denise Silvestro, at Pocket Books, whose skillful guidance helped me through the first rough draft and beyond. It is good editing, after all, that allows an idea to blossom into worthwhile reading.

And finally I wish to thank my family and friends for their support and encouragement, particularly my soul mate and cook, Mike, son Shane, and Chad, who sacrificed their time doing extra chores so that I could steal another hour to write.

This book belongs as much to the people I've mentioned as it does to me. It is as much their venture as it is mine.

# CONTENTS

# INTRODUCTION

When Brad, a California flight team paramedic, was thirteen, his mother was stricken with a heart attack at home. He remembers someone calling the ambulance, and standing back to watch as the emergency medical personnel moved in to try and save her.

"They rushed into the house carrying their medical bags, and began doing all these procedures I didn't understand at the time. The ambulance was sitting outside, its red light spinning, and though I was scared, I was struck by the drama of it all. I knew then I wanted to do this for a living."

Brad's mother died en route to the hospital, but even that didn't dim his interest in emergency medicine. Instead, the trauma seemed to solidify his burgeoning commitment to saving lives.

"My father was a volunteer with the local fire department, so I began hanging out with him, where the crew taught me basic emergency medical skills. By seventeen, I had worked my way into a rescue squad program, then on to paramedic training with an ambulance crew."

Today, at twenty-seven, Brad flies with a helicopter airlift program based in northern California. Married to a nurse, he says he cannot imagine being part of any other career field.

His dedication and lifelong fascination with emergency medicine are characteristic of the hundreds of nurses, paramedics, and pilots across the country who are part of this relatively new mode of patient transport. *Flight for Life* is about them, why they chose this occupation, and how they feel about their work.

The air medical industry began, at least in this country, in the early 1970s when forward-thinking doctors, nurses, and hospital administrators recognized the advantages of using aircraft for rapid transport of critically ill or injured patients. (Australia, by contrast, has been doing this for years, with their "Flying Doctor" program.)

Physicians refer to the time it takes to reach and treat such patients as the "golden hour," sixty minutes that can literally mean the difference between life and death. It can sometimes take ground ambulances that much time or longer just to reach a patient. A helicopter can fly in and out within minutes, to places inaccessible to ground crews. With the helicopter, highly skilled people and advanced equipment are brought directly to the scene.

There are currently more than 230 helicopter medical flight teams operating throughout the United States. Many are hospital-sponsored, others funded by state government, and a few independently financed. Samaritan AirEvac, for example, in Phoenix, Arizona, the first—and busiest—medical helicopter program in the country, is a division of Samaritan Health Services, one of the nation's largest nonprofit health care systems. Instrumental in developing the criteria for patient transport used in other flight programs, it has four helicopters, averaging 331 round-trip flights a month.

More typical is the air ambulance service in Asheville, North Carolina. Like most smaller programs, it has only one helicopter and a flight team composed of full-time and part-time nurses, paramedics, and pilots who work together in groups of three, on rotating twelve-hour shifts. Twenty-four-hour-a-day coverage is provided, 365 days a year. Hospital-based and funded, the MAMA (Mission Air Medical Ambulance) flys an average of 450 times a year, over a 250-mile radius.

Calls requesting patient transport come in from outlying hospitals, physician referrals, ground ambulance services, law enforcement, fire protection, and forestry service agencies.

Once dispatchers for the helicopter program are contacted, the pilot on duty is notified so that weather conditions can be closely monitored. If weather is questionable, affecting the safety of the flight, the pilot has the final say in approving or denying a transport. The patient's condition and circumstances are not relayed to him so that he can make clear-headed, objective decisions rather than reacting emotionally to the patient's critical need for service.

The medical director for the helicopter program can override a pilot's decision to fly if he thinks the transport is unnecessary, but that seldom happens, say flight teams. As a rule, it is the pilot who makes the determination, since safety—and the weather conditions that can affect it—are primary factors in any helicopter medical flight program.

While waiting for the pilot's approval, the dispatcher—usually based in or near the hospital's emergency department—seeks out the physician in charge of the ER and his staff to let them know a flight may be imminent, so that preparations for patient care can begin. When a transport is okayed, the dispatcher then relays a message by beeper to the flight team on duty, and the pilot and crew prepare for takeoff. Radio contact between flight teams and the emergency department physician of their home-based hospital is maintained as frequently as possible in order to receive directions for whatever medical procedures and drug treatment prove necessary for the patient during the transport. When radio contact is lost or temporarily interrupted and a doctor is unable to provide patient care instruction, the flight team is on their own in making these crucial decisions.

Not every patient is a candidate for an air ambulance. Specific guidelines for patient transport are followed, with flight crews normally responding to only the most serious cases—multiple injuries, for example, head and spinal cord trauma, cardiac and respiratory problems, high-risk pregnancies, severe burns, and industrial accidents. Other criteria include whether the patient's condition warrants speed, ability to withstand a ground transport versus airlift, and the necessity for a higher level of care than what's available at the scene or hospital site.

Cost to the patient for airlift service varies widely from state to state. Fees can range from as low as seven hundred dollars in the Southeast to four thousand dollars in the West. That is air time only, excluding medical procedures before, during, or after the flight. Nationally, charges average $1,433 for a fifty-mile transport, compared to two to four hundred dollars for a ground ambulance.

Flight program directors give several reasons for the difference in price, including the fact that air medical programs are considered the "new frontier of emergency medicine." Thus they have no standarized fees as yet.

In the beginning, hospitals that instituted flight programs saw them as good public relations, as well as a way to compete with ground ambulance transport services and generate income. Since health care is reimbursed primarily on the basis of charges, patients who were transported by helicopter generally required long-term, more expensive in-hospital care, and so accumulated the most charges. That was fine for income, but the expenses of operating the flight program were greater than most hospitals anticipated. At Memorial Mission Hospital, for example, where the MAMA crew is based, total cost to operate the helicopter program, including crew salaries, maintenance on the aircraft, and educational outreach programs, averages more than a million dollars a year, with a $300,000-per-year deficit. Unless the program brings its patient transport fees in line with costs, it will continue—as do the majority of hospital-based helicopter flight programs—losing money.

In the meantime, private and government-backed insurers balk at paying the true cost of rotorcraft services. A medical director for a helicopter program in northern California says Medicare is a major contributor to program deficits because they have no set reimbursement policies. They might pay a hundred on one claim, a thousand on another. As a result, hospitals that provide the flight service and do not get adequately reimbursed must absorb the inevitable losses that follow.

In a 1986 survey, forty-seven out of fifty-one services contacted said they had experienced revenue losses. Three reported a break-even. Only one had made a profit.

In 1992 the medical air flight industry remained in a state of flux, with program directors agreeing that hospitals need to reevaluate their programs and decide if the public relations benefit and status of having an in-house helicopter program are worth the operating cost.

Flight crews say the big bucks involved in operating a helicopter medical service are not reflected in their salaries. In fact, hospitals do not differentiate between in-house nursing personnel and flight teams. Flight nurses—R.N.s who must have a minimum background of two years in critical care or emergency care medicine—are paid the same as any other nurse employed by the hospital.

In 1991, 48 percent of flight nurses nationwide earned $35,000 and over, while 42 percent earned between $30,000 and $35,000, for an average annual income of $34,400. Paramedics, considered by some in the industry to be not as highly skilled as nurses, even though they are required to have eight hundred hours of training, earned on average $26,300. Pilots earned between $35,000 and $40,000 a year, a far cry,

INTRODUCTION

they say, from what they can make flying for private business.

So why do they enter this relatively underpaid occupation where on any given day they run the risk of watching people die before their eyes? Why flirt with the dangers of flying and the pitfalls of never knowing what will happen in an often uncontrolled—and uncontrollable—environment?

"I can be a nurse anywhere," says a member of a Houston air care program, "but as a flight nurse, I've got the added excitement of flying, plus the satisfaction of knowing that occasionally I can save a life."

"The adversities of flying are forgotten when a patient's family comes by and thanks you for all that you've done, even when they've lost a loved one," says a Cincinnati, Ohio, chief flight nurse. "It also becomes a way of life. We develop long-term friendships with our fellow team members. They become our family."

Others say they love the challenge of dealing with technically difficult patient care and the decision-making process that determines a patient's fate.

"There are not many jobs in which you can hold a person's life in the palm of your hand," says a flight paramedic.

There is little turnover—less than 2 percent overall in 1991—and most hospitals have waiting lists for nurses and paramedics who want to fly.

Yet misconceptions about the job run rampant, both inside and outside the profession. Many flight teams say they are perceived as the hospital's "redheaded stepchild," whose roles are not taken as seriously as in-house medical staff. On the other hand, there is a certain amount of jealousy from emergency personnel who feel the flight team gets *too* much attention from the hospital's public relations department, the media, and a fawning public who don't understand that patient care is a team approach involving many skillful hands. There are also territorial problems with ground transport crews and smaller hospitals who see their patients being "stolen," derisive remarks about "glamour jobs," and an overall feeling that these are "fly-boys and -girls" who get little of the work and all of the glory.

Politics are another source of conflict.

In a large Texas town, one flight crew reports that if there is an accident within the city, they are not contacted by the local fire department "because their program director hates our program director. So the only people who wind up using us are those in outlying counties. And no one says anything about it because it's so political."

All of these facets are covered in *Flight for Life*, beginning with a typical working day in the life of a flight crew in search of a patient, and continuing with topics as diverse as on-the-job perceptions and fear of flying. Along the way, I have allowed the flight nurses, paramedics, and pilots, as much as possible, to speak for themselves, telling their own stories. As a result, this is *not* a definitive study of the medical flight industry, but instead a glimpse into the human side of what it's like to be a member of an air flight team.

To meet the crews, I traveled throughout the country, from North Carolina to California, from the streets of New York City to the rural back roads of the South. Despite the geographic diversity involved, I hoped to find some common ground among them.

# INTRODUCTION

I learned that while various flight teams do share similar problems and characteristics, their experiences with patients are heartbreakingly unique. Everyone had a "flight from hell"—where anything that can go wrong, does. Yet each circumstance was different, each ending unpredictable, and each person's response to it as personal as his or her outlook on life, death, and everything in between.

As a whole, I found that flight crews are among nursing's most intelligent and resourceful employees. No one is harder on them than they are on themselves. Despite their strict standards of professionalism, they are their own worst critics. It is one of their most vulnerable traits, tending to make their jobs more difficult.

Their saving grace is a sense of humor, blackened by the somberness of what they do for a living, and never far from the surface.

"Me a trauma junkie?" says a respiratory therapist who flies with a Charlotte, North Carolina, team. "Yeah, I guess I have a penchant for blood and guts. I've always liked it. Now, *my* blood, that's different. That scares the hell out of me!"

"One of our crew members had twelve flights in a row in which his patient died," says a Charleston, South Carolina, paramedic. "We called him 'Reaper Twelve.' His partner was 'Reaper Six' because he only lost half a dozen."

Anonymity was promised to flight crew members who were willing to share their stories, and except in cases where permission was granted to identify team members, I have kept that promise. In some instances, locations are switched to further protect identities.

*Introduction*

My goal was to write a book that would provide a behind-the-scenes look at a profession filled with good days and bad, lives saved and lost, courage and fear, humor and pathos—life and death captured within the confines of a space no bigger than a closet.

In the process, I have attempted to explore the attitudes and feelings expressed by flight crews everywhere when the helicopter comes down and the doors swing open.

"All we want people to understand," says a North Carolina chief flight nurse, "is that we're not healers from the sky, nor are we fly-boys who get our kicks from getting on TV. Just because we're flying in a helicopter, it doesn't make us glamorous, or mean that we're better than anyone else. This is transport service—not hero service. We're humans who screw up from time to time, who follow the same limitations as everyone does. The only difference is, we have to try hard every day to overcome that, for the sake of the patients who depend on us for their lives."

Marie Bartlett Maher
*Ashville, North Carolina*
*1992*

"A six-year-old boy looked up at me
   and said, 'Are you a flight nurse?'
I told him yes.
He had just lost his eight-year-old sister in a car
   wreck.
'If I had some money, I would pay you,' he said.
'For what?'
'For bringing my sister to the hospital.' "

—Crystal,
flight nurse

# FLIGHT
## FOR LIFE

# 1

# *The Search*

*"We're not flying in because we're bigger and better, but because we're faster."*

—Chief flight nurse,
MAMA crew

IT IS MONDAY MORNING, LATE SPRING, AND GREG Lathrop is looking for a dead man. Not here in his cramped office at headquarters for Mission Air Medical Ambulance (MAMA) in Asheville, North Carolina, where he is chief flight nurse, but thirty miles away, at a river, where he, paramedic Benny Coleman, and helicopter pilot Martin ("Marty") Beckman are preparing to fly.

The call came in at 8:35 A.M. that a kayaker, missing since the previous day, still had not been found. According to the report, a thirty-three-year-old man from Greenville, Tennessee, wearing no helmet or life vest, overturned in the water Sunday afternoon, made it safely to a rock, then reentered the rapidly flowing water to retrieve his kayak. His friends, watching from the bank, said he surfaced once, then disappeared. Rescue squads, volunteers from local fire departments, and other agency representatives combed the river all day Sunday and into the night, to

1

no avail. Efforts to find the man resumed at daybreak Monday, with a request for the MAMA helicopter team to conduct an aerial search. Perhaps from the air they would spot something rescuers on the ground below had missed. A few years earlier, when the flight program began, calling MAMA was tantamount to admitting the emergency ground crew couldn't do the job. At the least, there was a certain territorialism between the "fly-boys" and the ground crew—a "this is my space and you don't belong here" kind of attitude.

Fortunately, most of that animosity has since disappeared, thanks in part to new management, and in part to the flight crew's concerted efforts not to swagger in and out of a scene call. Instead, they attempt to respect everyone's role in emergency medicine. However, dispelling the notion that helicopter flight programs are "glamour jobs" is an ongoing public relations problem for flight teams everywhere.

"We keep emphasizing that we're not bigger and better," says Greg, "we're just faster."

Diplomacy is one of Greg's many strong suits in his job as chief flight nurse. That in itself—the promotion to chief—is no small achievement for someone who was only twenty-five at the time. In fact, he was the youngest chief flight nurse in North Carolina when he got the job in 1987, and one of the youngest in the nation. Now, at thirty-two, he retains his youthful looks—a mop of thick, dark curls, black mustache neatly trimmed. An early Burt Reynolds in a burgundy flight suit, only taller, better built, with a little more muscle and a lot more hair.

It is not his looks, however, but his voice and manner that convey a sense of authority. Whether describing a scene call or an issue of national importance, he has an intense, articulate style that captures the listener's attention and leads one to conclude that as the years progress, Greg is destined to become an imposing old man.

Yet like everyone, he wrestles with private demons. On bad days he's mercurial, moody, carting around his fears and angers like unwelcome guests who won't leave.

"When Greg gets like that," says one of his crew members, "we know not to push him, or bring up certain problems."

"There are times I want to knock the shit out of him," adds another colleague, more to the point. "But then we go out bowling that night and it's all forgotten."

Greg says he got into nursing for the challenge, which is why he began his career in emergency room medicine and intensive care. He likes dealing with problems that need fixing, particularly when the problems are bad and the fixing requires immediate, aggressive action.

"Most flight nurses are like that," he says. "You have to be a certain personality type to make it in this business—somewhat cocky, confident, sure of yourself, able to make quick and accurate assessments. And you have to understand why you're in it. I'm not in this for the flying, I'm in it for the very sick patients who need my help and my on-the-spot decisions. That's where I find the constant challenge."

\*     \*     \*

On this Monday morning, he is standing before a wall-length topographical map, arms crossed, lips pursed, listening as his immediate supervisor, Skip Myers, and pilot Martin Beckman, their fingers pressed against the map, discuss which part of the river should be explored. Beside him is paramedic Benny Coleman, Greg's partner on today's run.

Next to Greg, Benny appears even smaller than his actual height of five feet seven. A former paramedic with emergency medical service, Benny waited two years before a full-time opening appeared with the flight crew, due to so little turnover in the job. Despite a slow southern drawl, he has a quick, sharp mind and an easygoing manner.

"Are we gonna have room for food?" he wants to know.

"Yeah, let's get our priorities straight," jokes Greg.

Skip Myers, white-haired, bearded program director for the MAMA crew, temporarily turns his attention from the map.

"Benny," he remarks over his shoulder, "you got a hollow leg, did you know that? You can eat more than three men put together."

"Marty says I've got worms," Benny replies.

"I believe it, I *believe* it," says Skip.

Marty Beckman is concentrating his pilot's eye on map details, ignoring the comments. Tall, slender, and slightly balding, he is quiet, almost shy by pilot standards. A South Carolina native, he has more than twenty-four years of flying under his belt. The area over which he'll be taking the crew poses no particular hazards, but low-flying searches, requiring intri-

4

cate maneuvering of the aircraft, can be difficult. Yet no one would know that from his nonchalant expression.

"This is my opinion of where to look," says Skip, returning to the map. "The French Broad River blends into the Tennessee around Knoxville. And here's where Spring Creek comes in. It's a large body of water below a bridge. A hell of a drop. I read an article on that river. You might want to go to the state line and work your way back. I'd say about a six-mile stretch.

"All he had on," Skip continues, referring to the lost kayaker, "was a pair of shorts and a T-shirt. No helmet, no nothing. I guess he just decided to take a ride down the rapids." He sighs audibly. During his twenty years in emergency medicine, he's become well acquainted with people who push their luck beyond the safety limits.

"We're not expecting to find a live person," Greg announces to no one in particular. The silence that ensues implies he's probably right.

The MAMA team does not, as a rule, conduct aerial searches, but has made an exception this morning because other rescue efforts have failed and because a request for their presence was made. It is their mission to pinpoint the kayaker, make sure no medical treatment is required, confirm the death, and be on their way. An ambulance standing by would then transport the body to a hospital morgue, where a medical examiner would officially determine the cause of death.

Twenty minutes later, Marty at the helm, the MAMA team prepares to lift off from its helipad at

Memorial Mission Hospital near downtown Asheville. It is the sixth year of operation for MAMA, a program that began in 1986 when North Carolina awarded Mission Hospital a $350,000 grant to implement the service. Since then, the team of eighteen paramedics and nurses, plus four pilots, have made more than two thousand patient flights throughout a seventeen-county region in western North Carolina, with no accidents or major mishaps.

Marty cranks the BO105 twin-engine helicopter, capable of traveling up to 150 miles per hour, its rotor blades whirling in the clear mountain air. The ship is a deep burgundy color, with the familiar large white logo MAMA imprinted on its side. Inside the helo is a narrow seat for Benny, next to Marty. Directly behind the pilot's seat is Greg, whose large frame nearly fills the remaining space. All three men have inserted earplugs to diminish the roar of the engines, and each has donned a headset and hand-held mike for relay of radio transmissions. Once airborne, there is no other means of communication, short of mouthing words or using sign.

The only room left is taken up by a stretcher, its length manuevered into the narrow confines of the ship's rear. Medical supplies, including airsick bags, line the aircraft walls, a tribute to the crew's utilization of space. The flight team's uniform, a one-piece zip-up jumpsuit with a Velcro belt and numerous cleverly designed pockets, is geared for easy storage of small but necessary items.

Suddenly a red light appears on the console.

"Gremlins," Marty announces. "We'll have to shut down."

The hydraulic block warning indicates a potential problem with engine number one. When the light comes on, it means the system is automatically switching to engine number two. It is part of the ship's checks and balances to ensure a safety backup in case one engine fails.

In the silent cockpit, as Greg and Benny patiently wait, Marty thinks the light, an urgent bloodred against the black console, simply needs resetting.

Mechanic Karl Esbenshade, whose job it is to ensure the safety of at least three lives (four if there's a patient on board) and more than a million dollars worth of machinery, checks the hydraulic system and concurs with Marty's assessment. He resets the light and climbs down from the aircraft.

Once again the engine cranks, spinning rotors, mesmerizing hospital workers nearby. It seems that no one on the ground is immune from the inherent fascination of a helicopter rising up or coming down, no matter how many times they've seen it take off or land.

"MAMA One to Madison, can you read me?" Benny says into the mike as the aircraft lifts off and upward. On this flight, as the crew glides past carpeted green mountains en route to the river, it is Benny's turn to handle communications.

"Madison Unit 300," he continues, "we're about ten minutes out. Do you need us to land, or what's the plan?"

Greg interjects, wanting more details before they arrive.

"Some good things to confirm," he tells Benny,

"are: Have they found the kayak? What color shorts was he wearing?"

Benny shakes his head in frustration. Radio static and other traffic vying for air space is interfering with his transmission.

"I can't hear a thing," he says. It is a common problem during medical flights, particularly in the mountains, and can lead to loss of contact at critical moments, especially when a patient is on board and the crew is needing instruction from physicians at home base. When that situation arises, the crew must make all their own decisions.

The radio crackles and Benny listens while the dispatcher's voice returns, relaying information from one of the rescue squad volunteers on the river below.

"He was traveling toward Tennessee wearing a white T-shirt, multicolored shorts—" Once again, the transmission becomes a garbled web of unintelligible voices.

"There are a lot of shallow places in this river," Benny says, talking to Greg through his headset. "I guess we're gonna sweep the area. There's a man post set up. Hey, I can see it right there!"

On a side road at a bend in the river, among a cluster of thick pines, are ambulances, pickup trucks, and several canoes. Other boats form a line across the water, part of a grid search that involves sectioning off parts of the river, dragging each part with a sweeper, then moving on to the next section. It is a tedious, time-consuming job, but remarkably effective in covering nearly every square foot of the river's bottom.

As a former ground crew paramedic and rescue diver, Benny knows that most drowning victims in a river become ensnared on something: a rock, or a tree limb that literally holds them under. Unless swift currents dislodge and move the body along rapidly, it tends to stay within a ten-to-fifteen-foot radius of where it submerged.

But this river—the 217-mile-long French Broad, flowing westward into Tennessee—is well known for its rapid, unpredictable currents. Even here, at the search sight, on one of the calmest, most shallow parts of the river, tiny whitecaps puncture the water's surface, indicative of the river's full strength. One of its earliest victims, more than a century ago, was a black child, son of a runaway slave, whose mother tried to swim her way to freedom. She escaped, but the child was swept away by the river's currents.

Marty must first guide the helicopter down the river's path in order to seek out potential hazards that can hamper a low-flying search. Greg and Benny are his extra eyes and ears on this preliminary look-see. They are scouting specifically for threadlike, hard-to-detect power lines strung across the river.

"Those are definite no-nos," says Greg. "You don't want the aircraft to hit one, accidentally or otherwise." He counts three sets of lines over the six-mile site. Benny and Marty do the same, coming up with identical numbers.

"Go back around this way," Greg tells Marty. "I thought I saw a spot of color, a bright green." He reaches over and slides open the door, his view of the river now unimpeded. A blast of fresh air enters the cabin.

Marty dips and turns the helicopter, hovering at times less than thirty feet above the river's surface. Suspended in midair, it shudders like a frightened child.

"I think that's a trash bag, or maybe part of a tent," says Benny. "But you never know." A second look confirms that it is, indeed, floating refuse.

Moments later, Benny, his neck craned downward, points to an object he just spotted.

"Is that a rock? That's a funny-looking rock to me."

Once again, Marty takes the aircraft down for a closer look. And once again, it's a false alarm, the tip of a boulder that appears curiously orange as it rises from the water's surface.

A mile farther, the water turns muddy, glistening like brown glass in the morning sun. An abandoned car sits nose-down on the riverbank, its hood touching the water, as though the driver simply parked, got out, and swam away.

After an hour and a half of searching first one side of the river, then the other, Greg concludes it is unlikely they will find the kayaker today, dead or alive. Without a word, Marty turns the helicopter homeward. They will not resume the aerial search unless there's a significant lead from the ground crew, who will continue dragging the river.

"There are so many places he could be," says Benny.

On the way back, Greg tells Benny about the new house he and his wife just purchased. She's a former flight nurse who used to work for him, but is now director of the emergency room at Mission Hospital.

Their first night in the house, an elderly woman two doors down was murdered in her kitchen by someone she had hired to do chores.

"Now I've got to think about installing burglar alarms," says Greg.

"I know what you mean," says Benny. Moments later, his thoughts return to the missing kayaker and the flight crew's lack of success in spotting him.

"Think they'll find him?" he asks Greg.

"Doesn't look good," Greg responds.

Two days later, after nearly one hundred searchers were unable to find the Tennessee man believed to have drowned, his body emerged not far from where he had plunged into the chilly river water to retrieve his kayak.

Sitting in his office, Greg reflects on the search and his team's role in responding to the call. The cost of flying the helo and its crew to and from the river, an amount absorbed by the hospital, will total more than seven hundred dollars.

A wasted use of time and resources? That, says Greg, depends on your point of view.

"Nothing dramatic took place," he says, choosing his words careully. "No victim was found and there were no pseudoheroics. We basically just flew in, buzzed around, and flew back. In that sense, we provided a service to the rescue ground crews. So I can't say it was wasted time and effort. But by our standards, it was a very mundane flight."

Yet that, he admits, is part and parcel of all emergency medical service. Not every scene can result in heart-pounding rescues. Not every call can save a life.

But every so often a crisis occurs in which life and death do hang in the balance, where high-level skills are called on and tested, and where speed in getting to the patient is of the utmost, critical importance.

It is this type of call, say helicopter flight members, for which they studiously train, patiently wait, and which they truly believe makes their job worthwhile.

# 2
# River Rescue

*"It was no longer my decision. I was either going to come out of there or I wasn't. Then I knew, when I started moving, I was going to live."*
—Slim Ray,
kayaking specialist

THE TRIP BEGAN ON A GLORIOUS NOTE. A CLOUDLESS sky, temperatures hovering in the mid-eighties, a cool green river, on a lazy summer Sunday.

Fred "Slim" Ray, a forty-three-year-old kayaker who had just returned to North Carolina from a two-month boating trip to Colorado, had been looking forward to this for a long time. He was part of a group of kayakers making their first run down the Green, a turbulent river located at the southeast end of Henderson County in the Blue Ridge Mountains. Wild and surly on its upper end, it winds its way through gorges so narrow and steep that treetops on opposite sides of the river nearly touch. Even experienced boaters like Slim consider conquering its formidable rapids a notch on their belts.

Not only an expert kayaker, having paddled in South and Central America, Europe, Siberia, Canada, and the western United States, Slim was a profes-

13

sional river instructor, a photographer, an author of two books on canoeing and river rescue, and a trainee in wilderness emergency medical care.

What brought him to western North Carolina was the combination of mountains and rivers, both of which allowed him to pursue his passion for outdoor sports.

Originally from Pensacola, Florida, he came north in 1980, first commuting the ten-hour journey from Florida to North Carolina just to ride the rapids. Before long, he found the trip impractical, deciding to relocate instead. Divorced, with no children to support, he landed a job that fit his tastes and talents at the Nantahala Outdoor Center in Bryson City, North Carolina, working as a river guide on the waters he had grown to love.

Exceptionally tall—six foot seven—with salt-and-pepper hair and a smooth, unlined complexion that makes him look younger than his mid-forties, Slim acquired his nickname from a coworker who couldn't remember Fred's proper name.

"I was a motorcycle mechanic at the time," he recalled, "and one of the guys I worked with could only get my attention by yelling, 'Hey, you, Slim!' I was the longest and leanest one there, so I knew it was me. From then on, it stuck."

With a degree in law and international affairs, Slim could have just as easily been a corporate nine-to-fiver, spending his days driving a BMW, conducting business on a cellular phone. The problem was that he didn't like the constraints or the pressures of an office job.

Says his friend and fellow kayaker Gordon Grant:

"Slim has a dignified presence about him, a stoic, almost lordly manner, much like a nineteenth-century British commander. Yet he thrives on freedom and independence. I'm not sure in what era he belongs. But I think he was born out of his time."

Gordon was along on the trip that July day.

There were eight others, including Slim, many of whom were making their first run down the Green. Leading the group was twenty-five-year-old Tom Visnius, who had run the dangerous sections of the river already, but only after earning the reputation for being one of the most powerful paddlers in the country.

En masse, the group was formidable: strong, experienced, highly skilled kayakers who wanted nothing more than a pleasant ride and the temporary thrill of confronting nature on its cutting edge.

Dam-controlled through Lake Summit, the Green River's water level was predictable enough. However, the same could not be said of its narrow, hidden hazards. The first three miles, just below the dam, were relatively benign, providing an easy warm-up for the group.

A little after 2:00 P.M., they approached the "Gorilla," the first in a series of three major rapids classified as severe. Located in an overall region called the "Narrows," it is a part of the river that few people enter. Tall pines and leafy elm, birch, and maple hug the banks, silent witnesses to the raging torrents of water that burst over room-size rocks, then boil and cascade their way downstream.

Here, in the Narrows, rapids are defined as posing "extreme risk of life," according to the American

Whitewater Affiliation. These are serious, Class VI waters that require "scouting," which means a boater should make a visual check for hazards, then plan the run stroke by stroke.

Though Tom Visnius served as lead man, each kayaker was expected to scout his own rapid before deciding to enter.

Heading into the Narrows, Slim reflected on the trip so far.

"I was thinking about what a great day I was having," he said, "and how strong everyone looked in the water."

Reaching the Gorilla rapid first, Tom decided to run it without scouting. He'd been down it before and felt confident he could ride it out. The others, some of whom wondered if Tom was pushing it a bit, got out and walked their boats to the calmer water below. Slim chose to run it and went through with no problem.

The "Nutcracker" was the next rapid down. Again, Slim rode its whitewater walls without incident.

By now it was nearing 3:00 P.M. The final rapid in the series was dead ahead—"Sunshine Falls"— regarded as technically difficult even by the pros.

"To run it safely," explained Gordon Grant, "you have to go diagonally from left to right over a fifteen-foot drop, instead of going straight down. At that point, you come into a small eddy. There you must turn and run another five-foot drop to get out of the eddy. If you fail to make the diagonal move across the first part of the rapid, the boat will land vertically onto a rock shelf below."

One by one, four of the kakayers entered the chute

that would take them into the raging current. Each ran the rapid with little problem and triumphantly appeared below. Slim was next in line.

His reputation on the river, according to Gordon, was that he took an analytical approach, seldom taking risks before weighing all the pros and cons.

"He has a real taste for adventure," said Gordon, "but he's not what we consider a risk seeker. He uses good judgment, which makes him well respected."

Paddling furiously, Slim plunged into the river's left side above the fifteen-foot drop and began the diagonal drive toward the eddy. Powering across the top wave, he thought, "I've got it made. I'm right there."

Suddenly the boat swung off the drop and flipped over, striking the rocks in one swift, bone-crushing blow.

Slim was trapped inside, unable to move or breathe.

He could feel the water's dense weight pressing hard against his back and lower spine, so hard, the pain so intense, that for a moment the world around him turned a bright crimson.

"Oh shit," he thought, his mind struggling to absorb the impact of what had happened. "I'm in trouble!"

Seconds later the boat inched forward, then began washing down. Once he was moving, he knew that unless he hit his head on a rock, he probably wouldn't drown.

But the pain . . . awesome. Overpowering. Like a big-wheel truck had parked itself on his back.

"It was then I started thinking about survival," he said. "I had another drop to go over, a five-foot ledge, and despite the pain, I was glad to be moving."

Down below, Gordon Grant and the others witnessed the run.

"We saw Slim's boat disappear upside down in the spray," said Gordon. "About two seconds later his paddle floated out, followed by his kayak, still upside down. Then Slim surfaced beside it as it swept over the second, smaller drop. I could hear him shouting in pain and I knew there was a serious problem."

Gordon grabbed a rope and threw it toward Slim as he floated downstream. The others watched, horrified, as Slim's helpless form drifted farther away. Elizabeth "Bunny" Johns, a fifty-year-old Georgian with more than thirty years' experience in kayaking, moved in behind Gordon to help.

"I've hurt my back!" Slim gasped. He reached for the rope, but missed. By now he was almost too weak with pain to move. For the first time, he wondered if he was going to survive after all.

"Gordo, I don't know if I can hang on to the rope," he said.

But Gordon, wading deeper into the river, tried again, summoning all his power and strength, as though the force of his energy could somehow be channeled to Slim.

"You can't quit now," he said, urging Slim not to give up. "Come on, man, you can do it!"

This time Slim caught the rope. Gordon and Bunny gently reeled their friend into a nearby shallow eddy.

"I'm really hurt. I can't feel my legs."

Gordon and Bunny realized that for Slim—known for his tight-lipped stoicism—to admit he was badly injured must indicate a problem worse than they thought.

"Okay, Slim," said Gordon, "tell me how you feel. Are you warm enough?"

Gordon began a primary survey of Slim's arms and legs, looking for any type of response. Four of the other paddlers waded into the pool to see what they could do. Someone removed the length of foam blocks, four inches thick, that line the inside of kayaks and tore them into strips to form a bed. Smaller pieces of foam were torn into triangular shapes to brace Slim's neck. A life vest was placed around his neck as a supporting structure.

"The idea," said Gordon, "was to allow Slim to float, but minimize any movement."

"At one point," said Bunny, "we tried to pick him up as a unit, but he couldn't stand the pain. We knew the water level was dropping, so we raised him up on the rubber blocks and pushed him toward the right side of the river, near the bank."

Meanwhile, Tom Visnius and John Woolerd started the forty-five-minute trek that would take them up a steep trail to a parking area where they could drive to a phone and call for medical help.

It was 3:50 P.M., less than an hour since the group had paddled into Sunshine Falls.

As the water level continued to drop, the self-appointed team of rescuers, led by Gordon, monitored their patient, continuing to stabilize his neck and covering him with plastic trash bags to prevent further heat loss.

While Gordon, a trained emergency medical technician, kept track of Slim's physical condition, Bunny offered comfort and support, remaining at Slim's head, holding his hand, talking to him, letting him know what was going on around him.

For the next hour and a half, Slim lay motionless in the water, a time he describes as "the longest moments of my life."

"I was trying everything I could use to control the pain, including self-hypnosis," he said. "When that didn't work, I'd scream my head off."

At about five-fifteen, Tom and John arrived back with the first of the rescue squad volunteers who had responded to the call.

Gordon was worried the rescuers, in an effort to get Slim out as fast as possible, would inadvertently cause additional harm to Slim's back. That was no reflection on this particular rescue crew's skills, but more a fear based on Gordon's past experience with medical emergencies in general.

"We insisted on having a first aid leader identified and assigned within their group," said Gordon, "before anybody was allowed to move Slim. And I told everyone to slow down, stay cautious."

A few minutes later, Rick Mott of the Henderson County rescue unit arrived and took charge, getting fluids into Slim's system through an IV and helping package Slim onto a backboard and into a Stokes litter—a basketlike device that allows for easier handling of patients than a standard stretcher.

Then Rick made a decision.

"We need to call the helicopter crew," he said.

Gordon shook his head.

"A helicopter's not coming in here," he said.

"There's no way. Look around. Where are they going to land? It's just not safe."

Mentally he had already prepared himself for a long and arduous hike out of the gorge getting Slim to an ambulance. For Gordon, this entire day was taking on a surreal quality, like watching a film over which he had no control.

Then he glanced at Slim, noting the deep lines of pain etched across his face. Rick saw it, too.

For a moment the two men stood silent.

"We'll call MAMA," said Rick.

More than sixty miles away, the Mission Air Medical Ambulance is returning from a routine patient transfer to Winston-Salem, North Carolina, from Memorial Mission Hospital in mountainous Asheville. The weather is clear on this Sunday afternoon, temperatures peaking into the eighties as MAMA flies into its home base in Asheville.

On board are flight nurse Linda Marlow, thirty-seven, and paramedic Rieley Bennett, thirty-five. At the controls is Paul Calloway, a forty-five-year-old Vietnam vet who has flown as a bush pilot for the U.S. Forest Service in California, Idaho, and Arizona. Flying rugged terrain is nothing new for him, which is why he likes the mountains—it provides a bit more of a challenge.

Of the three, Rieley Bennett is perhaps the most laid-back. A native of western North Carolina, he has been a paramedic for eleven years, first working in emergency medical service with ambulance crews. In his off time he is a volunteer fireman. Married and the father of a three-year-old, he is solidly built, prematurely balding, with large, expressive brown eyes, a thick handlebar mustache, and an unmistakable knack for putting people at ease. At home in a crowd of "good ole boys," he can just as easily hold his own with anyone, anywhere.

"He's like a good ole boy, but smarter, with a lot more common sense," is how someone once described him.

Flight nurse Linda Marlow has somehow managed to carve out a career in nursing for the past fourteen years, despite the fact she has five children, including two-year-old twins. A former homemaker, she went into nursing because she wasn't sure what she wanted to do, fell in love with the profession, and worked her way up from emergency room nursing to the flight team.

Along the way, she has paid a heavy price. Not only is her time with her children limited, but her husband tells her she devotes way too much to the job. In fact, her career has been a sore point in their marriage to the degree that before long, the couple will temporarily part.

"It's hard for him, not being in medicine, to understand what this is all about," says the soft-spoken blonde. "I come home from work and want to share with him a big case I've handled, or a scene call, and he can't really relate. He thinks it's just a glamour job."

It is close to 6:30 P.M. when the crew touches down in Asheville, and Linda and Rieley are tired. Both are scheduled to get off at 7:00 P.M., and they are ready—after an afternoon spent cramped inside "the bird"—to head home. Linda's husband is waiting,

22

kids in tow, at the heliport pad to take the family to church.

The helicopter lands, and the trio, Linda, Rieley, and Paul, begin the cleanup procedures necessary after each call—from straightening out the ship's interior to restocking supplies. It will take them fifteen to twenty minutes to complete their chores. Ten minutes into cleanup, their beepers sound. The message from the dispatcher is urgent.

"We were told we were needed at the Green River gorge," recalls Linda, "and we were like 'Man, what's going on out there?' "

"Looks like a kayaker with possible critical injuries," says Paul, sharing what few details he has gathered. On most scene calls, there is usually little information going on, especially for the pilot, who cannot base his decision to fly on the type of patient and injury involved. Instead, he decides to fly according to weather and other safety factors, in order not to risk the lives of either patients or crews who depend on him for transport.

Still, all three flight members know that this is a different type of call, one that will challenge their skills and endurance. For Paul, maneuvering the helicopter in and out of the narrow, steep gorge will test him to the limits. Yet he is ready—almost eager—to go.

"This is the kind of flying I've been trained to do," he says.

Linda and Rieley, their weariness replaced by an obvious excitement, have climbed back into the helo and are strapping on their seat belts. Glancing out the large expanse of window in her jump seat beside the pilot, Linda hopes that maybe this time her husband, who went on to church without her, will understand.

Rieley has canoed down the Green River but has never been inside the Narrows. Now, headed in that direction, he realizes he is about to view it from a whole new perspective—the tops of the trees. He wonders where in the hell they can land.

Linda wonders the same.

"We knew nothing about the landing site," Paul recalled later. "But from a general safety standpoint, we look for a good entrance and exit, at least a hundred feet square. What concerned me about this particular site was the lack of a safety margin. Anytime you go into a situation like that, you have to hope that the worst won't happen, that an engine won't quit, for example.

"Then you work with the terrain the best way you can. I'm an intuitive pilot. I get a feel for the wind currents, the general slope of the land. It's like a dance, and you have to find the rhythm, your place in it. After that, it usually works out. At least, you must go in assuming that it will."

Paul flies up the river gorge, makes a U-turn, then heads back toward the kayakers, who are difficult to spot through the thick, overhanging trees. It is their colorful helmets—small dots of red and yellow beneath a thicket of leaves—that finally pinpoint their whereabouts.

"All I can see is a little hole in the trees," Rieley tells Paul, "but it looks like that's where they are."

On the preliminary flight up the gorge and back, Linda and Rieley have both scouted for power lines and other hazardous objects, reporting anything they see to Paul. It is during this time that Paul must decide whether to cancel the flight because it presents too much danger, or commit to go in. Once that commitment is made, there is no turning back, and the crew knows it.

Rieley and Linda, still unsure about Paul's decision, look around the cabin for loose objects, latching everything down that might pose a risk during a turbulent entry. It is an effort to minimize whatever danger they can.

"If we hit anything at all," Linda says to herself, "it's all over."

"Don't move," says Paul into the radio mike. "Don't unbuckle your belts. Don't even breathe until I tell you it's okay. We're going in."

Making his approach, Paul spots several onlookers standing on the rocks below not far from where he wants to set down.

"Get those people out of there," he radios to the emergency ground crew below. His plan is to fly over the site, turn around, and come back so the aircraft will be above the rapids, several hundred feet from the patient.

"I decided, yeah, I could put that thing down on a rock, but I didn't want to approach from upriver in that kind of terrain, because it's nearly impossible to fly out of. So we turned around and came down the gorge instead."

Coming in toward the kayakers, Paul can see there are still people on the riverbanks. His temper flares.

"I said get them the hell out of there!" he yells into the radio, addressing the ground crew below.

His destination is a large, misshapen rock right in

25

the river, bringing the craft under the tree cover first, then sliding it onto the landing area, no more than twenty by twenty feet in size. It will take quick thinking and courage, considering this kind of terrain is inhospitable to all types of aircraft.

The scene before him reminds Paul of another tricky flight he made, this time in the snowy mountains of Colorado. A woman was in labor at Pike's Peak, eleven thousand feet above sea level. Her husband had gone for help in a snowmobile and it broke down, whereupon the local rescue squad—who found him—called for air transport for his wife. It was dark by the time Paul arrived, and he had to slide the helicopter into a space so small, there was only three feet of room on either side when he landed—on top of fourteen feet of snow.

At least here, at the Green River, the water level has dropped. Controlled from Lake Summit, the river rises around noon, when extra water is released so boaters can enjoy a better ride on the rapids. Around 6:00 P.M., the dam is shut, causing the waters to recede. Had they arrived an hour earlier, Paul's proposed landing site would have been three feet underwater, making an air rescue virtually impossible. Even now, once the aircraft lands, the crew will be completely surrounded by water.

Linda, absorbed in her thoughts, is watching the trees whisk by as Paul lowers the helo.

"Man, those trees are *close*!" she says to Rieley.

"I hope you've got your life insurance paid up," says Paul, overhearing her remark.

Linda reaches up and fingers the small, gold guardian angel pin she wears on her flight suit collar. It always makes her feel better, knowing it's there.

A study in concentration, Paul gently sets the aircraft down on the rock near the river's edge. It immediately dips to the left.

The ship's tail end is too heavy to balance on the rock, so Paul lifts the bird up, moves it forward three or four feet, and sets it back down. It wobbles like an oversize toy. Paul tries the maneuver again, and again. On the third attempt, the helicopter settles onto the landing.

"Okay, you can hop out now," Paul says to his crew.

Rieley leans out the doorway, notes that two-thirds of the skids are still suspended in midair, and turns to Paul.

"No way!" he says. "I'm not climbing out on that. There's eight to ten inches of space where the skids aren't even touching the rocks!" He is worried that the helicopter, perched in its precarious position, might topple into the water.

"Then put something under the damn thing," Paul replies calmly.

Unable to argue with that, Rieley climbs out, grabs a log floating in the river, and kicks it into place under the skids.

All the while he's thinking, "I can't believe I'm doing this."

Linda, whose concern is now for the patient they are about to rescue, begins preparing medicine and supplies, even though, at this point, she isn't sure what injuries are involved.

Paul cuts the engines on the aircraft, and all three

flight members climb onto the rock, no bigger in size than a small bedroom. From where they are standing, they cannot see or hear the kakayers below. But they can hear the roaring rush of the rapids and, closer in, feel the needlelike sting of its spray.

Paul's job completed for now, he waits on the rock while Linda and Rieley tackle their next challenge—getting down below. It will involve fording the river near the helo, hiking down the bank paralleling two rapids—the Nutcracker and Sunshine, respectively—then walking chest-deep through the swift-flowing river below in order to reach the right side of the river, where Slim and his friends are waiting.

From where the aircraft is sitting, it is about a hundred yards to the lower end of Sunshine, with no easy route in between. This is one of the most narrow parts of the river, high, rock-strewn banks wedging the water inward until it becomes canyonlike in its depth. Once at the foot of the rapids, whoever goes down must help decide how best to transport Slim back to the aircraft.

Rieley, studying the scene below him while marveling at the power of the river, asks Linda, "Do you want to go down, or do you want me to go?"

It is not a question rooted in heroics, but part of a logical decision-making process that involves doing what is most advantageous for the patient.

It is Linda's belief that physical strength and manpower to get Slim up to the helicopter should be the determining factor. She tells Rieley to go.

"I'll have everything ready here by the time you get back," she says. Though she doesn't verbalize her fears she is worried that if she tries, and fails, to

28

swim the river's currents, she might become another patient.

Setting off on his way to the kayakers below, Rieley is having his own doubts about this part of the rescue attempt.

At first he has no trouble. Dressed in his burgundy once-piece flight suit, he is warm and comfortably attired, other than his shoes. They are not made for walking in waist-high water, on rocks that feel like greased poles.

"What if I slip and fall and wind up injured, too?" he is thinking as he gingerly works his way through the swift current and over the slippery rocks.

Two steps later, he is down.

"Oh great! This is great!" he says out loud, recovering his balance. "The rescuer has to be rescued!"

"You're looking good!" yells one of the EMS ground crew below as Rieley comes into view. "We'll give you a nine-point-oh on that one!"

"Very funny," Rieley mutters. He is surprised, however, that he got this far across without additional mishaps.

Nearing the group of kayakers, emergency rescue squad, and Slim's inert form still floating in the water, Rieley spots a rope someone has strung across the river and grabs hold, pulling himself along.

Slim can hear his approach from behind.

"I was flat on my back, looking up, and all of a sudden this kind face appears," Slim said later, "and this deep country voice says, 'Hi! I'm Rieley Bennett and I'm a paramedic.' I felt a great sense of relief that finally I was going to get out of here."

By now, Slim has already been stabilized, so

there's little additional medical treatment required. Rieley takes a brief history of his patient and makes a quick assessment. To his trained eye, the kayakers have done an excellent job improvising with what they had on hand. The ground ambulance crew—for whom it was no easy task to hike into the Narrows—have also performed their jobs well, placing Slim in the Stokes litter and stabilizing him with a neck brace and intravenous fluids. He is fully "packaged"—ready to transport upstream.

Now if the group converged at the scene can agree on how to accomplish that task.

When Rieley convenes with the EMS rescuers and the kayakers who pulled Slim to safety, they are having a heated discussion about which route up the river is the best one to take.

"We can run a transverse line and rig a harness," says one of the EMS crew, "but it will take about thirty to forty-five minutes."

"We can pick him up and actually carry him," says Gordon. "Sure it means more effort, but we'll get him out of here a lot quicker. We've already got a path cleared up the right side of the river."

"I don't know," responds the EMS paramedic. "I think we ought to run this line."

Rieley hasn't seen Gordon in thirteen years, but he remembers him from a boys' camp they once worked at together, and he trusts Gordon's judgment. Glancing toward Slim, he can tell he's in great pain. He also appears slightly cyanotic (bluish discoloration of the skin indicating poor circulation). Not a good sign. They need to work fast.

Gordon's plan means going upriver, above the aircraft, then downstream to a pool of water where three empty kayaks, lashed together, can be used as a float for transporting Slim, secure in the Stokes basket, right to the helicopter's door. It also means carrying the tall and lanky Slim a farther distance upriver, a move that—at least to some of the rescuers—doesn't make sense.

"We have several options," interrupts Rieley, playing devil's advocate, "and we can decide to work together until we reach the best one. But I caution everyone to be careful and take their time, because if we drop Slim going out, it's all over for him."

While the discussion continues, Linda and Paul are standing on a boulder above the rapids, straining to see what's below. Bystanders—summer hikers and other boaters on the river—have returned to the scene after being told to move when the helicopter flew in. Paul and Linda use the onlookers' knowledge of the river to ask them questions, hoping for details on Slim's run down the river.

Linda knows that time is critical because Slim has already been in the water two to three hours. As a result, he can develop spinal shock, or hypothermia, followed by his blood pressure dropping dangerously low.

Paul is concerned, too, for the aircraft is not parked in the most stable position. And he still has to get his crew, the patient, and himself safely home. He climbs past Linda over a large boulder to get a better view of the river that has, in one swift moment, changed Slim's life forever.

Paul has flown in Vietnam, fought forest fires from the air, and survived a major crash that, ironically—

in view of Slim's injury—broke his back and immobilized him in a body cast for nearly a year. But boating down this river is one thing he'd never do.

"Slim must be crazier than I am," he says to himself.

On the river below, Rieley is mustering his diplomatic skills to convince the group to follow Gordon's suggestions.

"We've got enough people here to form a relay line to get Slim across," Rieley says. "And the path along the bank is ready. Why don't we just carry him up there?"

He gets a momentary perplexed look from an EMS crew member, followed by silence. A few seconds later, everyone agrees the kayakers' route probably is, after all, the best way to go. Differences of opinion are now cast aside and a solid alliance formed.

"When we get to the top," explains Rieley, "we'll set up two lines, and we'll pass him along on the Stokes litter, hand over hand. Then we'll re-form the lines and continue till we get him across.

"Let's do it right," Rieley cautions again, "with no panic, no hurry. Everything uniform."

For the next twenty minutes, Slim, writhing in pain, is hoisted to the river's right edge, one hundred yards uphill along the steep bank, past the waiting flight crew, and MAMA, perched unsteadily on the rock.

"I wasn't worried they'd drop me," Slim said later, "because everyone was being very careful and cautious, but besides my pain, I was concerned about the helicopter getting out of there safely. There have been problems in the past with helicopter rescues, which is why I preach, in my river books, no transports by air unless absolutely, positively necessary. It's a conservative doctrine, based on the knowledge that poor communication and bad landings increase the risk that something will go wrong, along with unstable weather, darkness, and potential malfunctions.

"I thought, 'If we crash a helicopter on top of everything else . . .' "

He knew that playing the odds with the river, and losing, can spell death. Only a year earlier, his friend Rick Bernard, an expert boater, drowned in the Chattanooga River in Tennessee.

Rick was paddling a series of rapids when he slid under a rock. Slim saw his hand reach up and then someone throw a rope. But Rick missed it, and disappeared under the water. Moments later, his life vest floated out. The boat had been pinned under a rock and was folded over, the force of the current pushing Rick against the front of the kayak's cockpit rim.

For over an hour, Slim and a group of rescuers tried to extricate their friend, but the rope wouldn't hold around the boat. It took more than half a day and several efforts before the boat and Rick's body were finally freed.

Now it is Slim's turn to be carried up the river.

The eight-man team of kayakers and EMS personnel, led by Rieley, reenter the waist-deep water above the rapids, heading for the pool where three kayaks, lashed together to form a float, sit waiting. Slowly and gently, they place Slim atop the hand-rigged flotation device, then begin the push across the width of the river en route to the aircraft. There are two people on each corner of the kayaks, with a rope across the middle. Unable to keep their footing on the uneven bed of the river, they must alternately swim, then push their way across, using the rope for leverage. More than a hundred feet away, they can see Paul and Linda standing on a rock by the MAMA aircraft, waiting for their patient.

Incredibly, Slim—considering his tormented state—is apologizing to his rescuers "for all the trouble I've caused."

Linda, wading out to meet the group, is thinking of the flight out and the complications that might arise. There is a weight factor, for example, that must be computed each flight, for there is not only limited space on board, but a restricted amount of pounds the aircraft can comfortably handle. Even one extra person, or a particularly heavy load, can tip the delicate balance, diminishing the safety margin in lift-off. Slim and his Stokes litter are extra weight. So is a soaking-wet Rieley. So is she, now that she's entered the water.

"Don't you jump in and get wet," she calls to Paul. "If you do, we'll never get out of the river!"

As Linda reaches the group, she grasps for the litter that holds a cold and wet Slim. They are now almost alongside the aircraft.

"I'm hurting so bad," he moans.

"I know," she says. "But we'll have you under way soon."

Rieley gives her a quick rundown of Slim's injuries and condition. Paul hands her dry sheets and a blanket, and she wraps Slim warmly, for there will be no space inside the cramped aircraft to maneuver. Then she injects him with morphine to control the pain, plus another medication to combat nausea.

Paul cranks the helicopter's engines while Linda climbs inside, followed by an inert Slim in the Stokes basket. Rieley stays on the rock, clearing space and cautioning everyone to move back. Moments later, he, too, is on board and the MAMA doors snap shut.

Paul has memorized his technique coming into the river—a low, swift swoop under the trees, hovering over the site, a sideways turn, and a dip into the "hole" above the rock. He now reverses the moves, and the helicopter lifts off and upward smoothly, clearing the treetops. Rieley and Linda, both absorbed in the care of their patient, hardly notice they are airborne.

Then Paul's excited voice bursts into their headset.

"Yeah, man! I spent thirteen years in the Rockies doing this kind of flying! It's about time I got to try it here!"

Linda looks at Rieley and grins, her earlier worries forgotten. His matted hair and handlebar mustache are now dripping onto his wet flight suit. To her, he looks like a homeless pup.

She picks up the radio mike, ready to communicate with the outside world.

"This is MAMA One," she says to the emergency room dispatcher based at Mission Hospital. "We're about four to five minutes out. We have a forty-plus-year-old male who's been in a kayaking accident, cannot move his legs. . . ."

Slim's vital signs are reported and a rundown given of the drugs and medical treatment he's already received.

"Estimated arrival time," she says, "is seven to eight minutes."

While Rieley monitors Slim, she spends the next few minutes jotting notes on pieces of tape, then attaching them to the legs of her flight suit. Later on, she will assemble the individual pieces and use them to fill in her flight report. The details of who, what, when, and where are required paperwork for every scene call.

At the rescue scene, Gordon Grant and Bunny Jones are starting the strenuous hike out of the gorge up to the area where they have parked. From there, they will drive to the hospital to check on Slim.

Walking up the winding trail, Gordon is consumed by morbid thoughts about the river.

"I had these sudden waves of frustration," he recalled, "over the fact that we couldn't do anything more, and that it had happened at all. It comes down to an individual decision—whether to go into a rapid or not. We all know that, but it underscores my belief that you can't be too cautious."

The MAMA crew, nearing the heliport, are deciding how to code Slim's arrival. Code Green means no one is needed to meet them at the pad. Code Yellow means "wait till we shut down, but be ready to move fast," and Code Red indicates a true emergency—in which the patient is whisked out of the aircraft and into the ER, crew running at full speed. Even the helicopter's engines remain cranked in a Code Red, often referred to as a "hot unload."

The team decides to designate Slim's case a Code Yellow.

"We wanted to use caution in moving him," explained Linda, "and sometimes that doesn't happen in a Code Red because everyone's in such a hurry to get the patient into the emergency room. Also, his pain had subsided and he was more comfortable by then."

Inside the ER, Slim undergoes a series of tests that indicate a badly damaged lower vertebra, which will require the insertion of steel rods. He is told there is a chance he will not regain the use of his legs. In the weeks ahead, he will gather his strength from the support and encouragement of his family and friends: Gordon Grant, Bunny Jones, and others who believe in his courage and ability to meet the future.

At this writing, Slim's prognosis remains uncertain. He undergoes rehabilitative therapy on an outpatient basis, is working on a new book about canoeing, and he has every intention of reentering a kayak to ride the rapids again.

For the MAMA helicopter crew, the rescue had all the elements of a "good" call.

"I still can't believe we landed there," says Linda. "The only time I've had a bigger rush is when I sky-dived out of an airplane."

"Everyone worked together well, and everything clicked," Rieley adds. "Considering all the hazards and potential problems, we were also just plain, damn lucky."

It is 9:15 that same Sunday night, after the Green River scene call. Rieley is sitting in the MAMA head-quarters office, finishing up his part of the report. It's been a long, eventful day, and he is bone-weary. He knows that once the remainder of the crew learns of his dip in the river, he'll never hear the end of it.

(Sure enough, within days, he is tagged "Rescue Rieley" by his cohorts.)

Linda, still wired from the day's events, has headed home and wants to talk to her husband, share the excitement of what she's been through.

"Come here!" she tells him. "You've got to sit down and listen to this! You're not going to believe this place we flew in and out of. . . ."

But he is not responding. She goes to another part of the house and talks to her children instead, asking about their day. Sitting on the living room floor, legs crossed, she lets them climb over and around her, tugging at her playfully, as she wonders what price she pays for her career.

A few miles away, Rieley, his work at the office completed, enters his home through the kitchen. It is late, but his wife, also a paramedic, is there, waiting up.

"So did you have a busy day?" she asks.

"You might say that," he responds.

Her interested look now turns puzzled. "Why are you all wet?"

He describes the river rescue and his unexpected foray into the water.

"Hmmm," she says, "sounds like a pretty interesting scene call."

He is hungry, tired, and wants to change clothes. "I guess so," he says, heading for the shower. "But it's just another case. Who knows what might happen tomorrow?"

# 3
# Scene Call

*"You go out and people say, 'Oh, this must be a great job.' And it is. But it's also periods of horrific fear when you're up there and no one—not even you—knows what will happen next."*
                                            —Texas flight nurse

LIKE RIELEY BENNETT, MANY FLIGHT CREW MEMbers take dramatic scene calls in stride, accepting daily unforeseen events as simply part of their job description. For others, it is the uncertainty of not knowing what each call will bring that keeps them interested in how they earn a living. And for still other flight members, there is an element of fear, coupled with excitement, in being placed in situations they cannot control.

Emergency medicine, in all its facets, is built on the premise that unexpected things can happen to anyone at any time.

According to the National Safety Council, accidents are the leading cause of death for Americans aged one to thirty-seven, and the fourth leading cause of death for all ages. Motor vehicle accidents lead the way, followed by falls, then drownings. Persons under eighteen suffer the most accidents, males twice as often as females, particularly during the teenage years. In motor vehicle accidents alone, more than two thousand teens a year are killed on our nation's highways. Younger children, infants, and toddlers up to age three are the most likely victims of burn injuries and smoke-inhalation death from fires.

Those are the facts and figures. But flight crews see much more than that. Behind those hard, flat statistics lies the human element—the pain of seeing a child in agony from third-degree burns, the vacant stare of a grieving parent, the disbelief of sudden, unexpected loss, the emptiness of knowing that despite high levels of medical skill and experience, there are times when nothing, absolutely nothing, will save the day.

Some cases, flight crews remember more vividly than others. Some they never forget. . . .

It was 7:00 A.M. and we were scheduled to get off at 8:00. We got a call to meet at the scene of a residential fire, but by the time we got to the helicopter, we were told instead to go to the hospital. They were going to stabilize the patient and transfer her to a burn center.

We landed at the hospital about five minutes after a ground crew arrived with the patient. As soon as we walked into the emergency room, we could sense something wasn't right. Everyone was in tears. People we passed down the hall were visibly upset—unusual behavior for ER personnel who are accustomed to high-stress situations.

Then I got a whiff of an odor you never forget,

that of burned flesh. One of the most awful smells we encounter. I went into the room, and there on the bed was a five-year old girl, literally burnt black. Even the tips of her toes were burned off, exposing her bones. Her hands were so cooked, they had clenched into a tight fist position.

Yet she was still alive. No one could read her blood pressure because she had third-degree burns over 100 percent of her body.

Earlier that day, her mother had performed some kind of ritualistic burning of candles—white for people she liked, black for people she hated—and she left them in the child's bedroom closet. The girl was sleeping and woke up to a house in flames, her bed on fire. The mother was nowhere in sight.

My partner and I looked at the kid, then at each other.

"What are we doing here?" I said. "I don't want to fly this patient to a burn center. I don't even want to *deal* with this."

The ER doctor and our medical director were also in the room, performing various medical procedures. I remember thinking, "Please, God, don't allow this to continue. Let this poor child die. There's nothing in the world that can be done for her."

Then another doctor, a surgeon, walked in. He stood back and watched while the other two doctors focused intently on trying to save this patient no matter what.

"You know," said the surgeon, "this is a terminal injury. Physically, there is no way this child can survive."

It must have clicked, because one of the doctors suddenly stopped what he was doing and said, "You're right."

That's a difficult lesson for all of us in emergency medicine to learn. We have this hero-rescue image, and our job is not to fail. We *can't* fail, because when we do, it means somebody dies. Physicians are like that, too. It's very hard for all of us to accept the fact there are things that are out of our control.

We went across the hall where the mother was waiting, and the doctor in charge informed her that her child was doing to die.

"A burn center would be useless in her case," he said. The mother had little to say. Later she was charged with criminal negligence.

The transfer was called off and our services no longer needed. We were glad, though still upset. Normally we are a cool, collected bunch, but this was a horrible situation even for us. Here was a small child's body burned beyond recognition, yet still alive.

The child died shortly after we left her. When she expired, I think everyone in the emergency room breathed a collective sigh of relief.

Not all accident victims are children, of course. Sometimes they're not even human. But that distinction hardly matters to this nurse, caught between compassion for her patient and other "victims" at the scene, and a healthy concern for her own personal safety:

One of my first flights was a rural call in a small town in North Carolina. This man was driving drunk on a country road, late at night, in an area where horses were known to wander.

Just as the man was coming past a fence, three of the horses jumped over it and onto the road, striking the car. One of the horses came through the windshield and landed on the man's chest.

When we arrived by helicopter, we had to come into a pasture next to the road. Aboard was the pilot, a paramedic, and me. Paramedics are trained to look for safety hazards at a scene, while we go straight for the patient. So while we're approaching the scene, John, the paramedic, suddenly grabs my arm and says, "Whoa, Linda! Look at that!"

I peered into the darkness and could see three moaning, bleeding horses straight ahead. One was up and attempting to walk around. The other two were between me and my patient. I knew if I rushed in and spooked them, I could be trampled to death.

But I could also see the patient was in trouble—in fact, was going into traumatic arrest and needed an IV line in *fast*. By now, onlookers had gathered, and I told one of them, "I need a flashlight." Next thing I know, six big spotlights are focused on this guy's chest. We intubated him [placed a tube down his throat so he could breath] and did a bilateral decompression [a procedure that removes blood and/or air from the chest cavity, so the patient's lungs can expand].

And in the background I could hear this lady screaming, "What about the horses? What about the horses?"

I don't think they were taken care of until the next day. Meantime, we got our patient loaded in the aircraft and took off. He recovered nicely, but I never found out what happened to the horses.

Alcohol is a primary force in about 100,000 deaths per year, reports the Center for Disease Control in Atlanta. However, it is estimated that the figures are actually six times higher, since many death certificates do not list alcohol as the cause of death, and blood-alcohol level readings often take two to three weeks to confirm.

About 50 percent of motor vehicle accidents are alcohol-related, yet no one is sure how many injuries in all types of accidents could be avoided if people did not drink.

It is this conclusion—that alcohol abusers inadvertently victimize others through accidents—that frustrates and sometimes antagonizes flight crew members who witness, and then must deal with, its consequences:

We had a two-year-old child come into the emergency room with a gunshot wound to the abdomen.

She had been sitting on her father's lap, and a friend who was visiting picked up a .22 rifle and started fooling around with it. Both men were drinking at the time.

"I think I'll just shoot you," the guy said to the child's father. He thought the gun was empty, he said later, but it fired twice and hit the

44

little girl. One bullet went through her side, barely missing her lung; it nicked the liver and lodged in her spleen. The father was also shot, once in the chest.

We were standing in the emergency room when they were brought in by a family member who drove them to the hospital. The doors burst open and someone is carrying the child. Right behind him comes her father with a big hole in his chest, yelling, "Take care of her first!"

We got them calmed down, but couldn't locate a surgeon. The doctor on call had a gallbladder operation scheduled upstairs and didn't want to change it. So the child had to be transported by our helicopter team to another hospital that would do the surgery.

The stupidity on the part of the adults in her family was bad enough, but now she was victimized twice. The kid was dying, and the administrative part of the hospital appeared not to give a damn. We got a pediatrician to come by and check her, but by the time he arrived, the weather was turning bad, and we had only forty minutes left of good flying time.

We had to make a decision fast. We gave her two units of blood and loaded her onto the helicopter for a flight to another part of the state. They took her right in as soon as we got there.

She was in the hospital three weeks, but she finally fully recovered.

We got a call that an officer was down. He was standing beside a car, writing a citation, when a drunk driver struck the vehicle. The crash put a two-inch crease all the way down the side of the car. The officer technically died at the scene, but we had to transport him back to the hospital.

The officer's family was Italian, and two of his brothers were also police officers. I remember bringing them all into the waiting room at the hospital and trying to explain that we had done everything that was humanly possible.

As I walked away, I could hear the mother yelling at her two surviving sons, "You *told* me he was going to be all right! You *told* me you'd look out for him!"

And I wondered for a long time how they would survive the loss.

My partner and I were called to an auto accident on the coast of northern California. We learned going in that there was one deceased patient, three or four critical patients, and no local ambulance available to come to the scene.

So we were the first advanced life support team to arrive. It was also my first call, and I could feel the adrenalin pumping. As we were flying in, I looked to see what kind of vehicles were there—what type of injuries they might have caused. We landed, and Brad, my partner, went in one direction to check for those victims who were most critical. I went in the other.

The entire scene was a mess.

There were two cars—a van and a sedan. The couple in the sedan had been drinking and broadsided a father and his children in the van. No one in the van was killed, but they were all injured and would require surgery.

Then I walked over to the sedan. I had seen

dead people in the hospital, but never freshly killed people at an accident. It was a surreal experience for me. The driver, a female, was dead. The passenger, her husband, was very much awake, in pain, and wanting to know what had happened.

I had a moment of panic, like "Where do I go from here? What do I do? What can I say?" But then my training kicked in and I was okay. I treated him medically, as best I could, and we got him transferred to the helicopter. The ground crew had arrived by now and transported the family members in the van.

All the way back to the hospital, this man whose wife was killed kept asking about her. I knew that inside the aircraft was not the place to tell him she was dead. I didn't want him freaking out on me. But I didn't want to lie either.

So I said, "I'm not with her. Let's worry about you right now. We'll talk about the other later."

At the hospital, the family had been separated—taken to two different hospitals—and there were a lot of upset feelings over that. As a result, the mother of the family, who was not involved in the accident, had to run back and forth between two hospitals visiting her husband and children.

Eventually the survivors recovered, but it was a traumatic experience for everyone involved, including me.

My first night call was an auto accident in the middle of nowhere in California. The scene was a highway in a canyon, on a road at the bottom of the valley. It was like flying into a black hole. Our job, as crew members, was to make sure we saw obstacles that could potentially kill us—like trees and power lines.

We were making an approach into this darkness, and I couldn't see *anything*. The guy on the ground relayed by radio to us that everything was clear.

As we were getting ready to make our final touchdown, I looked out, and sure enough, there was a high-tension wire. We flew over it, but just barely.

It really angered me. Here we were, landing in a dark hole on the side of a highway, and we could have been killed, while the guys on the ground were telling us it was clear.

When we got on the ground, I went around stomping my feet, so glad to be on firm footing. In fact, I didn't want to leave.

The patient was a drunk teenager who had crashed into someone else. He injured his head, but it was uncertain whether or not there was serious injury.

It turned out he was some drunk punk who was verbally abusive all the way back to the hospital. What really made me mad was that we had risked our lives—literally—to pick him up. I also knew we would do it again and again, for other patients, because that's what we're trained to do.

For the neophyte flight crew member, learning to expect the unexpected at scene calls is one of the toughest assignments of all:

I had only been out of orientation a month. We heard there was a major pileup on a highway in Tennessee, and the closer we got, the worse it sounded. Someone said one hundred cars were involved and there were people with multiple injuries. I was getting more scared by the minute. Being new, I hadn't even had a *two*-patient flight before.

I kept thinking going in, "God, I wish I had a parachute. I'd jump right out of this bird!"

But when we got there, it all went like clockwork. Everything I had been trained to do kicked in.

At the scene there were ninety-nine wrecked cars, sixteen fatalities, with seven or eight additional people requiring transport. We had two helicopters there, plus an ambulance.

A major fog moving in had caused the pileup. It was still foggy, and hard to see coming in, like a huge cotton ball had dropped onto the highway.

Visibility was so bad, in fact, we had to land at one end and have patients brought to us from the other.

As we were headed out, the fog lifted as mysteriously as it came. Suddenly it turned clear and bright, marred only by the smoke rising from the wrecked, empty cars.

I got back to the hospital and told someone I had just been on my first flight call, a ninety-nine-car pileup, and they couldn't believe it. It was like, "Man, it took me three *years* to go on a call that big!" You'd think I had just won the lottery.

People inside the medical profession know what we mean when we say things like that. It means we finally get to use our skills and do some good. But those outside medicine don't see it that way at all. They think we're just "gore-mongers," or cold and callous. If they only knew what it was really like.

One of my most surprising experiences was a premature delivery in the helicopter, fifteen hundred feet in the air. The mother was only twenty-five, yet in her fifth pregnancy, and eight weeks premature.

We were called to pick her up from a small hospital in upstate New York, two hours prior to her scheduled delivery. The doctor was going in induce labor, but the hospital said they had no bed for her.

I thought this was the most absurd thing I had ever heard. Why induce labor with a premature child, and how could they not have a bed for a patient already in the hospital?

However, I didn't want to make waves, so I said, "Okay, whatever you want to do."

As we were transporting her back to our facility, she suddenly announced, "The baby's coming."

I said, "No, no, it's just shifting."

Then the infant's head appeared and the mother screamed, "Is it alive? Is it alive?"

So what began as a terrible flight turned into a wonderful experience, for the mother and the baby survived. And I felt I had played an important part in making it happen.

Ask flight crew members what type of case bothers them most, and almost without exception, they will say it is scene calls involving children.

"You can try to forget those cases," said a male paramedic, "but they always come back to haunt you."

Even the helicopter pilot, who seldom has patient contact, often gets drawn into the drama of rescuing a child from certain death. When the flight team's effort fails—as it too easily can in critical care—no one, not the nurse, the paramedic, nor the pilot, is left emotionally untouched. . . .

Treating kids didn't bother me so much until I had my own. One day we were bringing a child back who had a congenital heart condition and was in cardiac arrest, and I got this weird feeling that everything around me was dying.

I felt like crying all the way through the flight. Outside the aircraft it was a beautiful day with a crystal blue sky, but all I could think about was this absolute feeling of desolation.

The child went into intensive care and eventually died. I find it strange that I can remember few of the details about the case, only the overriding feeling of loss, and the knowledge I could do absolutely nothing about it.

The call came in that a child had been attacked by a lion at a flea market near Houston, Texas. I had visions of someone being totally mauled from head to toe.

When we got there—me as flight nurse, the pilot, and a physician flying with us—we had to go through double glass doors in order to get inside the building. Right at the entrance was the lion, surrounded by three police officers with rifles aimed at the lion's head. Just beyond that was the patient.

The animal was alive, but wounded.

It had been brought in by some nut who had set up a booth where you could have your picture taken with the lion. The man had closed the booth and was getting ready to leave for the day when the lion brushed past a table and knocked over a vase. The loud noise spooked the animal. At the same time, a mother and an eight-year-old girl were coming in through the glass doors. The frightened lion lunged at the child.

The beast caught the girl's leg in his mouth. Then chaos broke loose. A security guard ran up and shot the animal. It momentarily let go of the child's leg, but then it grabbed her by the hair, so that the top of her head was inside its mouth.

At that point, no one was sure *what* to do. If the lion was shot in the head, the bullet could strike the little girl, too. It was a tough decision. Finally the guard decided to shoot anyway. Otherwise, he determined, the lion would not let go.

He carefully took aim and fired. As the shot rang out, the lion released the child, fell down, got up again, and went back after the little girl, who was now sprawled on the floor.

The guard shot a third time, and the lion went down again, but still wasn't killed.

When I arrived I could see the child was beyond the lion's reach, but *I* had to walk within two feet of it in order to get to the child. I was scared about going in because I was wearing a red uniform and thought it might further arouse the lion.

As I was coming through the glass doors, I turned to a police officer and said, "Now look, if that lion comes at me, you *will* shoot him, won't you?"

He assured me he would.

As I walked past the wounded lion, it never took its eyes off me, never stopped growling.

I got to the child and began treating her while security personnel arranged an exit out the back way so we could carry her through on a stretcher.

As I was bandaging the little girl's head, I noticed there was a piece of scalp and bone missing about the size of the palm of my hand. I looked closer and could actually see her brain, with the membrane still intact. That meant no obvious brain damage, but I had another fear—that she would survive all this only to die from an infection.

I wrapped the skull and got an IV going. She didn't seem to be in much pain, but was scared and worried about her mother, afraid the lion would go after her, too.

I then talked to the mother, who was still hysterical, and told her a police officer could bring her to the hospital. There was no room on the helicopter for all of us.

During surgery—one of a series of operations the child underwent—doctors found they couldn't replace the original bone in the skull, so they used an artificial expander. Plastic surgeons performed several hair transplants, and the little girl eventually recovered beautifully.

The lion's owner was charged with mistreatment of the animal, violating city ordinances, and child abuse. During the trial, the eight-year-old told the courtroom exactly what happened, but her words were not nearly as eloquent as the hat she wore that disguised her injuries and her loss of hair.

This little boy, two or three years old, was bitten by a pit bull. Part of the child's face was torn off and he was pretty messed up.

We landed in a little town called Middleton [California], about thirty-five miles from the hospital, picked the kid up, and were on our way back when we got a call to return to the scene.

Someone had found a piece of the boy's facial flesh and bone and wanted us to come and get it.

We got the kid off-loaded and into the emergency room, and the pilot returned to the scene alone. The facial parts were handed to him in a plastic bag, and he brought them back to us.

The surgeon said he was glad to see it because on a child that young, it would be difficult to reconstruct the missing piece.

The plastic surgeons did an amazing job of putting the boy's face back together again, and he has returned to his family, perfectly normal once more.

Every time I walk through the hospital, I'm reminded of this case, and I'll tell you why later.

The kid was about sixteen at the time, under a doctor's care, taking medication for a strained neck from football injuries.

Just before the game that night, he took a couple of pain pills, felt a little stiff at halftime, and took two more. By the fourth quarter, he wasn't having much pain.

Toward the end of the game, he ran a play, and someone rammed him, hitting him in the head. The kid went into a huddle with the other players, ran another play, and was hit once more. This time he staggered back to the huddle, so they sent him to the sidelines.

He no sooner sat down on the bench when he started vomiting. Suddenly he toppled over, not breathing. An ambulance—parked on the side of the field—loaded him with the intent to bring him to the hospital, but the trip would take nearly an hour. The kid could be dead by then. That's when they called us.

It was a beautiful, clear night. As we lifted off, we could see the lights of the ball field in the distance, miles away.

We landed on the fifty-yard line, the stands packed for a home game, and I remember thinking "God, I hope I don't trip getting out of this helicopter in front of all these people!"

When we got to the kid, there were already several telltale signs of impending death. One pupil was enlarged and the other constricted way down. He wasn't breathing on his own, and he was "posturing" [abnormally stiffening and extending his arms]. We had to get him intubated *fast*.

John, my paramedic, and I got him intubated,

and he began to breathe better. We had him to the hospital by air in about seven minutes.

As it turned out, he had a burst vessel in the brain as a result of the head injury, and the medication was subduing it, until he got hit again.

The boy fully recovered and now works part-time at our hospital. I see him almost every time I walk down the hall.

A man and his son were in a lumberyard, and the father was riding a wood auger, a machine similar in purpose to a meat grinder in that it turns wood into chips.

The boy, about seven years old, was riding above his father when he slipped and got his ankle caught in the machine, pulling him in up to his knee.

It took forty-five minutes for the ambulance crew to extract him from the machinery, so we lost our critical "Golden Hour," that first sixty minutes after an accident which can determine whether a patient lives or dies.

You can save a leg if it's packaged right, and reattached within six to eight hours. So time is critical in that way, too.

We got to the boy, and the first thing the ground crew told us was how cooperative he was during the extrication. I knew that was a bad sign. When a kid is seriously hurt, and he's quiet and cooperative, that means he's losing the battle.

We checked him for color, responsiveness, and level of consciousness, which are even more important than a blood pressure reading in a child.

This kid was gray in color. And all he said throughout the flight was that his leg hurt.

We got him into surgery and he survived, but lost his leg. Maybe it will be easier for him to adapt than it would be for an adult. I say that because having one leg is basically all this kid will ever know.

The effect on me was that I discovered I don't deal well with kids getting hurt. I feel they haven't had their chance yet. And that bothers me a lot, for it's just not fair.

Flight teams learn to live with the knowledge that the outcome of any scene call is uncertain at best. Yet when tragedy strikes for no apparent reason, particularly when the victims are young, it is human nature to ask the perennial question: Why?

For this chief flight nurse there is another, even more disturbing question. Was her team's rescue effort worthwhile in the end? She says on this case she will always struggle for an answer. . . .

He was an eighteen-year-old college student on his way back to school after summer vacation. A car with a boat and trailer attached pulled out in front of him. The wreck removed most of his face—just peeled his entire face back.

When the ambulance crew arrived, he was sitting on the side of the road with all this blood and fluid pouring out of his face. Every facial bone was broken. But he had no other injuries.

My first impression upon seeing him was, "What a gruesome sight."

He was awake during the transport. We gave him oxygen and kept his airway open.

After numerous plastic surgeries, he is still legally blind and has a long way to go. I sometimes wonder if, in the long run, we really did him any favors. Or would it have been better had he died at the scene?

That's just my perspective and maybe I'm wrong, but bless his heart, people will always stare at him. He will never look like you and me.

On the other hand, he has a wonderful support system, a family who loves him, and who knows? He might accomplish great things.

I don't have the answer and I guess I never will.


Other scene calls inspire a different kind of question. Why do some people suffer traumatic injury while others, in similar accidents, walk away with hardly a scratch? And where do the miracles come from that are part and parcel of emergency rescue work?


This guy had every reason to be dead at the scene. He was working at a rock quarry in western North Carolina, and had climbed onto one of those pieces of equipment you see in your worst nightmare—a big funnel that narrows down to a tube for crushing rocks. This is the kind of machinery that takes boulders and turns them into gravel for driveways. You don't want to accidently fall into one.

But that's exactly what he did.

He was on top of the machine, working on it, when a rock hit him in the back of the head and pushed him into the crusher. The boulder then fell on top of him. So here he was, caught between a huge boulder above him, and grinding teeth below. Literally caught between a rock and a hard place.

For five full minutes, the machinery kept grinding, until someone realized what happened and turned it off.

When we arrived at the scene, he was still trapped inside the crusher, unable to move one way or the other. It took about forty-five minutes to free him, by getting a crane to lift the boulder.

Somehow, he escaped major injury. All he had was a broken jaw, which he sustained when the boulder fell on him!

We were called because of the potential for injury. You can't predict what might happen in those few minutes after he comes out of there and the pressure is relieved. He could have suffered a cardiac arrest on the spot.

We administered IVs, checked him out thoroughly, then brought him back to the hospital. Mostly our purpose was just to hold his hand. The experience had, understandably, scared the hell out of him. It scared us, too. We just knew he'd go bad on us before it was over. But he didn't. Who can say why?

It was about 2:00 A.M. on a summer day near Charleston, South Carolina. The man was boating by himself on a lake when he reached down to untangle a steering cable that had come loose. Suddenly he was in the water, watching the seventy-horsepower motor propeller coming straight at him. It sliced into his forehead, nose, mouth, and throat, all but cutting off his right arm.

He was wearing a flotation vest, so after about forty-five minutes, he was able to climb back into the boat. But there was no way to get the motor started. Instead, he began to paddle with his good arm. The next seven hours were a blur, he said, but he remembers holding his head down so he could breathe through the cut in his throat.

"I really didn't think I'd make it," he said later. "The bleeding wasn't bad, but I knew how seriously I was mangled."

In the meantime, his wife had become worried and went in search of him. A stranger at the dock offered his boat, and together they set off. They found him about a half mile from where he had begun the trip. His face was peeled back, his nose hanging by loose cartilage. He couldn't speak because of the nose and throat injuries, so he simply waved his good arm.

We took off in the helicopter, but it was so dark by the time we got there, there was no way the pilot could see where to land. To solve that problem, emergency medical service personnel and fire fighters who had been called to the scene formed a circle with their cars and turned on their headlights. We landed in the center of the circle.

En route to the hospital, inside the aircraft, we had to sit the patient upright so he wouldn't block his airway. His jugular vein was visible, along with his right arm's main artery. His tongue was cut and he lost most of his teeth, as well as much of his jaw. He was a ghastly sight.

At the hospital he underwent thirteen hours of surgery and was in critical condition for two days. When it was over, there was only a 50 percent chance he would regain the use of his arm.

But, considering his injuries, we thought it was amazing that he did so well.

Another boating accident nearly claimed the life of this young girl, but with courage and determination, and the help of her husband, she, too, beat the odds:

They were both nineteen, newly married, and had just bought an outboard motorboat they wanted to try out. This was a boat with a large motor and strong propeller.

She was behind the boat, on water skis, and her husband was tinkering with the motor. He revved the engine, but reversed it by mistake, and the boat went backwards, running over the girl.

The blade corkscewed her leg all the way up to her hip. By the time we got there, she was in shock. That is the body's reaction to trauma. In extreme cases, it can kill.

The emergency ground crew had already started treatment, so at first we didn't fully appreciate how bad it was. She had been placed in MAST trousers [an acronym for military anti-shock trousers], which help offset the effects of shock by pumping air inside the trousers, forcing blood from the extremities into the body's vital organs.

When we got to the trauma center, we began weaning the trousers off her. Since shock affects the entire system, deflating the MAST must be done slowly and carefully. As we prepared to lift her out of the garment and onto another stretcher, we could see the leg up close for the first time.

She had over seventeen fractures. And she was filleted every two inches, all the way up her leg, where the propeller blade had sliced. It took eleven of us to move her—twenty-two hands to lift the independently cut sections of her leg.

The accident occurred in fresh water, so I knew the chances for infection were good. I predicted she would die from that alone. At the very least, this was a serious, serious injury, and I was positive she would lose her leg.

She went into surgery at least thirteen times during the next five months. She had all kinds of grafts, did get an infection, but recovered. Therapy helped, though one leg will always be smaller than the other.

Every day, without fail, her husband was there beside her. He even quit his job and sold everything they owned in order to stay at the hospital and remain near his wife. I thought it unusual—and uplifting—to see that kind of devotion in a person so young.

Several months after the girl's release from the hospital, I was getting my hair cut and the stylist asked me what I did for a living. I told her I was a paramedic with a helicopter crew.

"Do you remember that case . . ." she asked, recalling the girl in the boating accident.

It turned out the girl was her best friend, and she went on to tell me the couple are still married, both working again, and doing quite well.

Usually we don't even know if our patients live or die. There's so little time for follow-up, and even if time allowed, we're legally bound not to interfere with patients after they leave our care. So it was gratifying to know how this one turned out. It's one of the few times I felt we had come full circle.

All flight crews say that once in a while, a "big" story comes along that makes them realize the true value of the work they do. This accident, on the Gulf of Mexico, jeopardized the lives of hundreds of people and resulted in millions of dollars in property damage:

"We got word that a petroleum plant near Houston had caught fire and multiple injuries were involved. Something had happened on the ship channel, and the reports we were getting stated that there were huge balls of fire and black funnels of smoke coming from this plant. A request followed to send everything we had.

We had two helicopters ready to go, and there were two others headed their way, plus several ambulance crews. When we arrived, the scene was chaotic. Someone on the ground was talking to us by radio, but he was unsure of his own location, so the directions he gave us on where to land were not reliable. To add to the confusion, there was black smoke everywhere. We couldn't even tell what was burning. Was it toxic? No one knew.

"Hold your breath," said the pilot, "We're going in."

Ashes were falling from the sky as we landed. Everyone was running around, so we determined from that the air must be okay to breathe.

As the flight nurse, I got out of the aircraft first. I took a few steps and heard this huge explosion. I spun around and the pilot was taking off—leaving me behind! I'm like, "Wait a minute! Oh shit! What do I do now?"

Later, he told me he had to lift off because of the danger the aircraft would blow up, killing all of us. He circled and returned shortly.

I found a police car, and they drove me around to another site where other aircraft were "hot-loading" [placing the patient in the aircraft while the rotor is turning, to accommodate, in this case, quick takeoff].

There were people everywhere, some wandering around in a daze, as though they were shell-shocked. It reminded me of pictures you see of people after a bombing, their clothing shredded, covered in soot and broken glass, looking like walking wounded. I worried they would step into the path of a rotor blade. People have been killed from walking too close to the helicopter at accident sites before.

Our pilot noticed two guys sitting in a pickup truck, watching the scene. So he called over to them and said, "Hey, fellas, I need your help. Let's get these people redirected. Gather them up and lead them down the road away from the plant. We don't know if this thing will go up again or not."

FLIGHT FOR LIFE

After that, it became an assembly-line process, loading patients, transporting them, returning to load more patients. We felt like a shuttle service. Most of them suffered burn and inhalation problems, some serious. There were a few fatalities. In all, we treated three busloads of injured people.

To this day, we still don't know what caused the explosion.

During those times when the outcome of a scene call surprises even the most experienced flight crew member, it can take the form of a small miracle:

We got a call about a bad wreck near Great Falls, South Carolina; an elderly woman was pinned inside her vehicle. En route, we heard she ran her car through a guardrail, which then went through the motor of her car, through her front seat, and into her back, impaling her on the spot.

We came down to a thousand feet and could see the wreck about three miles away. By the time we landed, the ground crew had removed the woman from her car and covered her with a huge pad.

I pulled the bandage down and looked. She was eviscerated [intestines protruding] from her abdomen down to her thigh. I mean she was *hurt,* critically. In fact, the impact was so severe that her panty hose had jammed into her belly.

We put her in the helicopter and got another IV started. She was bleeding so much that her blood resembled water, having lost its consist-

65

ency. I looked at my partner and just shook my head. There was no way she was going to make it.

By the time we got her back to the hospital, we had blood on our uniforms from our chests to our toes.

The emergency staff rushed her into surgery, and believe it or not, six months later she walked out of the hospital.

Even more amazing, she sent us a photo of herself after her recovery—and she was dancing!

# 4
# *Laughter, the Only Medicine*

*"Life does not cease to be funny when people die, any more than it ceases to be serious when people laugh."*

—George Bernard Shaw

FLIGHT CREWS SAY THE ONLY THING THAT KEEPS them sane on a job that's filled with death and dying is those occasional lighter moments when there's nothing else to do but laugh or crack a joke. Even then, it's a type of humor seldom shared or understood outside the emergency medical setting.

"Someone not familiar with medicine would think we're highly inappropriate if they could overhear our conversations," said a pilot who flies regularly with flight nurses and paramedics. "We'll be flying into a storm, the helicopter shuddering, and the crew will break out singing, 'I Feel the Earth Move Under My Feet,' or something just as silly. It's black humor, of course, but it's our way of dealing with the stress."

"Everyone we transport is really sick," said a North Carolina flight nurse. "So we know we have to get real serious about what we do. We just don't have to take ourselves so seriously."

They even have their own internal jargon—admittedly irreverant—to describe certain patient transports.

There's "FTD," for Fixing to Die, "GOMER," for Get Out of My Emergency Room, "selling air," for giving a patient oxygen, and "hanging crepe," when it's time to inform family members that a patient didn't make it. One flight crew jokingly calls their program "MED-U-SCARE."

"This is a job in which you can quickly become very grim," says a Texas chief fight nurse. "That's why there's a certain amount of joking around on a scene call. And everyone does it, whether they admit it or not.

"We may have just piled two bodies out of a car, or held the hand of a dying child. We need a method of blowing it off, so that it doesn't overwhelm us, make us crazy. Offbeat, even bizarre kind of humor is our way of doing that. We mean no harm or disrespect."

In recalling those all-too-rare lighter moments on the job, they are often poking fun at themselves:

You miss a step and fall out of the helicopter, or leave a critical piece of equipment behind. Our pilot once tripped and fell right on top of our patient.

We really ribbed him over that—told him how that must surely have inspired confidence in the family, who, of course, were standing there watching the entire scene. There are a few stupid things you have to learn to laugh about in this business, but most of all, you have to learn to laugh at yourself.

It was a hundred degrees that day and we landed at the scene about 11:00 A.M. I hadn't eaten all morning.

My patient was a motor vehicle accident victim who had been pinned inside his car, but was now freed and lying on the ground. I had a doctor working with me, so together we bent over the man and began intubating him, before treating his other injuries. It took us about forty minutes. By then, I was hot and sweaty and feeling light-headed.

I remember standing up and realizing I was going to faint. I leaned over on the doctor, and he says, "What are you doing? Get off of me!"

The TV crews and cameras were there—all three channels—and about a dozen police officers, plus numerous spectators.

I said, "Oh, I'm fine," Then I passed out.

In the background, I could hear someone scream my name, and my colleague—the chief flight nurse—came running over. He jerked my patient's oxygen right off his face and put it over me! Then he says, "Don't do this to me. Don't do this!"

I was trying to tell him all I needed was a little glucose under my tongue. The cameras were all around me, and Tom screams, "Get those cameras out of here! My nurse is hurt! Call a third ambulance!"

Somehow I must have finally made myself clear, because I felt a sugar cube under my tongue and I popped right up. Before long, I was back to looking after my patient.

That has to be my most embarrassing moment.

Getting the goods on pilots, and ragging them about it afterward, is one of the joys of working with a flight crew team, say nurses and paramedics.

"It's so much fun to deflate a pilot's ego," said one savvy nurse, "because it has so far to fall!"

We got one of those iffy calls where we weren't sure the patient needed a quick transport, but we had to go anyway.

At the scene, we waded through three cow paddies to reach the guy and get him back to the helo. Then the pilot says, "I can't get the engine started."

So we get the patient out of the helicopter and onto an ambulance that's arrived at the scene, while we continue doing CPR.

The pilot calls out, "I got it fixed!"

Then he says, "No I don't!"

Then he says, "Yes I do!"

My partner and I look at each other, then at the patient.

"He's going by *truck*," I said. "It'll be faster."

Sometimes a pilot isn't exhibiting incompetence as much as he is exhibiting an inbred charm that seems to go with the territory of flying for a living:

We land at a hospital to pick up this sick kid, who's not as bad off as we thought, but we get him bundled up and out to the helicopter. Our time looks great—we're right on schedule.

There's only one thing missing. Our pilot.

Most often he's standing in the emergency room drinking coffee to keep warm. But we look around, and there's no place for him to hide.

We look everywhere—no pilot. We finally page him. It goes out all over the hospital, "Will the helicopter pilot please return to wherever it is he belongs?" He knows he's in trouble when he hears that over the intercom.

Finally he comes slinking out to the aircraft. We're sitting there waiting, tapping our fingers, ready to go.

"What have you been doing?" we ask.

"Public relations," he says.

"Yeah, right." We know what that means. It means making time with the nurses.


We landed at a difficult spot with a new paramedic. It was a hot, humid, miserable day. We had to go by ambulance to the scene, because our patient was still inaccessible.

It took a lot of medical procedures to get him out and treated properly, and we all had dirt and mud up to our waists.

After we finished working on the patient, someone passed out drinks to prevent exhaustion. Suddenly the new paramedic says, "Don't you think we ought to take something to the pilot?"

Our rookie didn't realize this particular pilot was very capable of taking care of himself, even after we told him so repeatedly.

But the rookie wants to take him a drink anyway. So we all pile into the ambulance and head back to the helicopter. Across the road is our pilot, sitting under a shade tree, fanning himself, a pitcher of ice water beside him, and this little old lady who lives there waiting on him hand and foot.

"Never mind," said the rookie, "I see what you mean."

Sometimes, however, the pilot doesn't always have the situation under control:

Normally, when a birth is immiment during the flight, we're able to tie the patient's knees together, figuratively speaking, and run like hell to get to the hospital.

But this time was different. The patient was a nineteen-year-old girl several miles from our county. We had reached the county line when we heard over the radio that she was ready to deliver. And it was twins.

The first baby had just been delivered as we set the helicopter down. Since the ship loaded from the side, we put her in backward, with her back to us, so that she was facing the pilot.

As we took off, the second delivery was imminent. About two minutes into the flight, we saw her point to her stomach and push. I could see the bulge and knew the baby was coming. There was very little space to maneuver and I couldn't reach her.

At first, all that popped out was water.

Then I saw the pilot turn around and his eyes grow big. The baby was headed right toward him.

"Oh, my god!" he said. The helicopter took a sudden dive to the left, then banked to the right, as though he was trying to duck.

Seconds later, the baby just missed landing in his lap. I managed to grab it in time.

That episode, especially the horrified look on the pilot's face, gave us our laugh for the day.

By the same token, a fumbling nurse or an awkward paramedic can provide the comic relief:

It helps to know your environment. I once jumped out at a scene call and ran smack into an electric fence. I did a quick 360-degree turn and jumped back into the helicopter. Meanwhile, my partner and the pilot were sitting there laughing at me. They knew the fence was hot, but said they wanted to see how fast I could move.

In this instance the patient gets a laugh:

I lost my balance when I came out on the skids of the helicopter. We landed and the paramedic got out. I was following behind him when I slipped and fell.

"Oh shit," I said. "I broke my leg."

The paramedic helped me back inside the aircraft and told me to splint my leg while he took care of the patient. But I wanted to help, too. So I hobbled down to where he was with the patient, a man who was not too seriously hurt, wide-awake and alert.

This paramedic was always teasing me about something, and I knew he'd have a comment to make when he saw me.

Sure enough, he did.

"That's what you get for being a smart-ass," he said while leaning over the patient.

Suddenly the patient bolted upright and yelled, "But I didn't *do* anything!"

It took us several minutes to convince this poor guy that he was not the target of our conversation. When we got him calmed down, he thought it was funny as hell.

Flight teams are often called on to perform certain public relations duties—from attending community-sponsored events to promoting awareness of flight programs by conducting educational tours of their facilities. It is during these up-close encounters with the public that helicopter teams learn how much—or how little—their work is understood.

We keep a stupid questions list. Like when I tell people I'm a flight nurse, and they say, "How can you fly a helicopter and take care of a patient at the same time?"

Or: "Does this helicopter land in the water?"

"Yes, but only once."

One man, an observer at a scene call, was explaining to his son how various helicopter parts work and was doing an adequate job until he said, "And these are where they keep the machine guns, but I don't know why they have them on this helicopter."

Then there's always the guy who brings someone close to where we land and begins telling him about the machine when neither one of them knows the first thing about it. As in: "Oh yeah, those are the jet engines—the thrusters—and that's how all the boost comes out, and how it goes so fast."

But my favorite story is when we stopped at a

Kmart parking lot. We dump a certain amount of fuel whenever we land, so when we got onto the asphalt, there was a puddle of fuel around us.

This man comes running up, excited about seeing the helicopter, takes a lighted cigar out of his mouth, and squats down on the pavement.

"Ain't that fuel?" he says, pointing with the cigar, its tip nearly touching the pavement.

We all stepped back *real fast* and I heard the pilot mutter under his breath, "Yes, you dumb shit, it certainly is!"

You can tell if people are messing with you when they ask stupid questions. But if the closest thing they've seen to an airlift is a rerun of "Air Wolf" on television, you take that into account and try to answer their questions.

After all, most people think helicopters routinely fly over hills and blow up.

In this scene call, even the patient was confused about the helicopter, its role, and his part in the rescue:

We got a call that we had a patient with an aneurysm (a ballooning of an artery or blood vessel), which is very serious and life-threatening.

When we get there, he's not only standing up, but he's waving at us, directing us where to land!

The only thing we could determine was that he thought he was supposed to guide us, or that we didn't know how to land without his help. Or maybe he was a former air traffic controller.

Comments by flight crews about their patients that are not related to medical treatment are strictly controlled on the aircraft, for obvious reasons. Not only are personal remarks about a patient considered unprofessional, but no one wants to get sued or fired over a careless slip of the tongue. However, despite such diligent discretion, some things have a way of tumbling out:

We went into the mountains of North Carolina to pick up this 250-pound patient who was well endowed. It looked like she had a hundred pounds on each breast.

We were having to move her every which way we could to keep her comfortable when all of a sudden our flight nurse blurted out, "Those are the biggest tits I've ever seen in my life!"

It was only then she realized our radio mikes were open and she had transmitted her comment all over the airwaves. She was most embarrassed. And our medical director, upon hearing about it, was none too happy either.

Doctors who fly with the helicopter crew are not immune from the pitfalls—or pratfalls—that are part of patient care during air transports:

We went on a flight accompanied by an Australian surgeon completing a residency at our hospital.

As the paramedic, I was sitting on the bench in the helicopter doing primary patient care, and our flight nurse was talking to the doctor.

He wanted to know if we, or our patients, ever got airsick while flying.

The flight nurse goes into great detail to explain that no, that doesn't happen because we're so well prepared and it can be controlled with medication, etc., etc.

Suddenly the patient rises up—like something out of *The Exorcist*—and spews forth all over me, the flight nurse, and the doctor. We were coated from head to foot.

"This *never* happens," the nurse kept insisting.

But at that point, I don't think the doctor believed her.

We all ended up laughing about it. There's not much else you can do.


In fact, as this scene call shows, flight crews come to expect certain "mishaps" on board:


We picked up a girl suspected of a drug overdose and were taking her back to the hospital when our paramedic decided she needed a substance to counteract her drug intake.

However, certain reflexes in the body tend to come around when someone takes your drugs away, reflexes like throwing up.

By the time our paramedic got out of the helicopter, he was wearing everything from pinto beans to chocolate pudding. He looked like someone had hit him with a pie.

All he said when we teased him was, "I thought I felt something warm on my leg."

In this job, you have to walk around like you're accustomed to having vomit all over you. It's one of our many perks.

Sometimes a mix-up in communication is the culprit in a scene gone wrong:

We got a frantic call that someone visiting the Statue of Liberty had fallen off. So we get fired up, ready to go, ambulances standing by, when another radio transmission comes through.

"Uh, negative on prior instructions," says the now hesitant voice on the radio. "Somebody fell off a beer wagon *at* the Statue of Liberty. Cancel the call."

We picked up a patient who was shot, and then dumped in the middle of the street. He was wearing a prison bracelet at the time, indicating he was under house arrest, which means his whereabouts are constantly monitored by his probation officer.

As we were transporting the man by helicopter, it occurred to us that somewhere down below, there must be a very confused probation officer wondering where the hell his client was going at 150 miles an hour!

Not every scene call is so simple or straightforward. Amid the chaos of an emergency is the ever-present element of human nature, which often adds to the confusion:

This was one of my first flights. We went to a little oil town on the Gulf side of Mexico. The call concerned an Italian working for an American company, who had been hit by a train.

Mexico wanted him transported back to the States.

We took an interpreter with us, because it can be difficult getting information from foreign officials.

We landed near the military base about 10:00 P.M. The first thing I had to do was go to the rest room.

As I was coming out of the stall, I realized there was no door handle leading to the hallway. No matter how hard I tried, I couldn't get the door open.

I started pounding on the walls.

Across the hall, I could hear my flight nurse yelling, "Tom, what's wrong?"

"I can't get out of the men's room!"

I heard her laugh at my predicament. She came to the door, but she couldn't get it open either.

"I'll go find somebody," she said.

I leaned against the wall, waiting, and came eye to eye with this huge black spider of God knows what origin.

Now I *really* wanted to get out of there.

About twenty minutes later, my flight nurse found someone who could speak English, and they came back and opened the door.

So far, this trip was not turning out as planned.

We got to the hospital, assessed our patient, and prepared to take him with us. I went to the door to make sure we could get the stretcher through, calling out the only words I know in Spanish—"One moment, please."

I turned back to the patient, but he's gone. Disappeared—along with my flight nurse.

I ran down the stairs and came out on a floor where absolutely nothing looked familiar.

Now I'm starting to panic. I've lost my patient and my way around. And I can't say anything in Spanish except "One moment, please."

Worst of all, I've lost Sherry, my flight nurse.

I wandered around for what seemed like hours until I finally heard Sherry's voice. Thank God.

"Let's get out of here," I said. "Where's the pilot?"

"I don't know. I've lost him."

"What do you *mean* you've lost him!"

So here we go again, all over the hospital, no patient, no pilot. When we run out of places to look, we wind up in the subbasement, and there they are—the pilot, the patient, and this whole entourage of people, all of whom are yelling and screaming in Spanish.

We grabbed the patient and the pilot and ran out the door.

And if I never see Mexico again, it will be much too soon.


This flight nurse, working in Texas, learned a basic lesson, too: Don't worry about appearances, especially when somebody's watching. . . .


I'm from New England, so I'm not accustomed to living in an area where there are swamps and bayous. Plus, I don't like snakes.

On my very first flight, we got a call to respond to a major accident near a bayou, with the landing zone undetermined.

I had on a brand-new uniform, freshly starched, and new shoes.

When we arrived, our paramedic had to climb into the water to get to the patient, while I sat in the aircraft, thinking, "Good, let him bring the patient to me and I won't have to get wet." Then

I heard this voice behind me—my chief flight nurse—commanding, "Go to your patient."

"Surely she's not talking to me," I thought.

"Go *now*," she yelled.

No doubt about it, she was talking to me.

I stepped out carefully, with the water already up to my thighs, I started trudging across the bayou to my patient, and my expression is like, "Get me *outta* here before I step on a snake!"

The victim's truck had careened off a bridge into the water, and he was pinned inside. When I reached him, the paramedic and emergency service crew were already working on him, so I climbed on top of the truck, wishing I was somewhere else.

Then I saw my chief flight nurse frantically trying to get my attention. She was pointing to the camera crews who were filming from the embankment. I knew what that meant—"Get off that damn truck and get busy!"

From that day forward, I never worried about my uniform, the snakes, the swamps, or anything else. I just did my job.

But you can't forget about appearance altogether, as this flight nurse learned:

We went to the scene of an accident where a sixteen-year-old girl had a head injury. This was a big girl, and I had to move her breasts out of the way to listen to her chest sounds.

We're in the middle of a crowd—ten people deep—who are watching the scene as though they were at the Indy 500.

My mind is racing, afraid I've forgotten to do

something. Is the airway in place? IV line attached? We loaded her onto the stretcher and carried her all the way across the field in front of the crowd.

Just as we were getting her to the helicopter, I was feeling pretty smug about the professional way I handled the situation. Then one of my co-workers tapped me on the shoulder.

"Hey, do you think you might want to cover up her breasts?" he asked.

I had such tunnel vision about her medical treatment, I had forgotten all about common decency.

I thought, "Oh shit. I bet we'll be on the six o'clock news. Me, the crowd, and this naked woman."

It taught me a basic lesson: Remember the medical procedures. Then remember indecent exposure.

Even when following procedures to the letter, strange and unusual things happen on the job, as this flight nurse and paramedic team discovered:

We went to a small hospital in Kentucky to get this patient, and the doctor in charge of his case told us the man was "passing in and out."

I looked at my partner and she looked at me like, "What is he talking about?"

Then the doctor said, "Watch."

He put the patient on an external pacemaker, and the man passed out. Then he turned it off, and he woke up. He did it several times, with the man passing out and waking up.

The underlying problem was a heart blockage, which, amazingly, did not prevent him from daily activities. He said he even drove a car.

As we were taking him off the pacemaker, the doctor turned to me and said, "Do you think I can get one of these for my wife?"

# 5

# *Perceptions*

*"People tend to forget we are advanced, highly trained personnel who give careful, good-quality care. They think we just zoom in and zoom out."*
—Susan,
chief flight nurse

ASK FLIGHT NURSES AND PARAMEDICS WHAT THEY think is the biggest misconception the public has about their work, and the usual response is, "That it's a glamour job."

Yet the reality of what these people do for a living is much different from such public or private perceptions.

"It's hot enough to fry an egg on the tarmac, and feels like a hundred thirty-five degrees inside the helicopter," says an Arizona flight nurse. "I'm doing CPR on a patient, and the sweat is pouring down my face. I have the "rotor-wash" hairdo—sticking out in every direction—and my makeup has long since disappeared. I've had so much sweat across my face, I literally could not see. Meanwhile, I'm doing everything I can to protect the patient, not only from the harsh environment, but from whatever trauma he's endured."

84

Listen to Maggie, a pretty blonde from Houston, Texas, whose femininity cannot be disguised, even in a unisex flight suit: "It's true, this job can appear glamorous because of all the media hype. The cameras are on you at nearly every scene call. Then you step in the middle of a cow patty where the helicopter has landed, or go home covered in blood and muck, and you think, Yeah, this is glamorous, all right!"

In Anchorage, Alaska, Margaret, a chief flight nurse, says that in her region, the weather is always working against them.

"It is thirty below zero on a typical winter day in Anchorage. But fly across the inlet and it gets *really* cold. Fifty below or less! Even in transports, where we are simply moving a patient from one hospital to another, we have to deal with cold weather conditions. For example, when an IV line freezes up, it can be devastating to a patient who is already critically ill. So during winter, we keep an electric blanket on the stretcher at all times. It may sound like a minor thing to contend with, but it's not, because everything we do has potentially serious consequences."

Other areas in Alaska are so inaccessible, particularly at night when weather conditions worsen, there are times the helicopter cannot respond, even if it means someone, trapped in the remotest parts of the region, will lose his or her life.

That's a helpless, demoralizing feeling, says Margaret, but, again, an element of the job that must be accepted by the crew.

The truth is, flight teams confront disillusionment

daily, along with unmet expectations, hidden problems, and pitfalls that go beyond the flights themselves. Relationships with coworkers and other colleagues are an integral part of the job, but have their own built-in complexities. In-hospital nurses, administrators, and other emergency medical personnel often perceive the helicopter team as overpaid and underworked. Family life is often adversely affected by the hours and the stresses and strains of emergency flight nursing. Family members resent the time team members spend away from home.

And the public, unable to see beyond the glamorized version of the flight crew's role, is enamored, amazed, enthralled by the idea of combining dramatic rescues with flying the skies. One flight nurse, upon meeting her blind date, was asked for her autograph—along with a request that she change into her zip-up, flame-retardant uniform for the date.

"People think we sit around and watch TV, then jump in the helicopter and get *on* TV," said a North Carolina flight nurse.

In reality, the helicopter and its crew are frequently a patient's last resort. Recipients of airlifted flights are usually victims of the worst kinds of injuries, the sickest of the sick. When the helicopter arrives, their very survival is hanging in the balance, and it is the speed of the aircraft and the caliber of its crew that often determine their recovery.

Because the job requires such a high degree of skill and dedication, flight teams say it is particularly distressing when they are misunderstood by patients, the public, their colleagues, and at times, their own families. Too often, they maintain, they are perceived as either heroes or air jockeys—angels of mercy or "fly-babies"—in it for the guts or the glory.

Brad, a California paramedic, says, "We're here because we're willing to stick our lives on the line—literally—to be health care professionals. For me, it's the most advanced way I know to do my job."

And it is a job, he added, that "can tear you up if you're not careful."

"Most of the public will never see anyone die up close," said a North Carolina paramedic. "But we do, every day, sometimes three or four times a day. That tends to chip a little off your soul."

Yet all agree that despite the heroic measures they must sometimes apply, none are heroes. Nor do they want to be.

"It's like we land at a scene and people wait for the doors to open," said a Knoxville, Tennessee, flight nurse, "as though we're going to step out with halos on our heads. It's embarrassing."

"We're not goddamn heroes," said another flight crew member, angry at such a ridiculous implication. "We're just people doing our jobs, like everyone else."

"Maybe the real heroes," said a Texas flight nurse, "are the people who recognized there was a medical problem and called us in the first place."

Misconceptions aside, flight members find it difficult at times to handle the stress of working with critically ill patients. Burnout is common, and a "long-timer" is anyone who stays in the business five or six years. Even the greenest rookie soon learns that every call, and every patient, extracts its price, both in the air and on the ground. . . .

*Marie Bartlett Maher*

I was new to the program and we were on our way to Jefferson City, Tennessee. We had a bad flight that day—a lot of turbulence—which made me nauseated. So I was sick when we arrived.

The scene call was a five-year-old child who had fallen into a pond and drowned. We worked on him and got a heart rhythm back, loaded him up, and put him on the aircraft.

During the flight his heart stopped beating and we almost lost him. We knew he probably wouldn't make it as soon as we arrived on the scene.

I was feeling worse by the minute—a combination of the airsickness and the helplessness I felt toward this child, whose life was slipping away before us.

I turned to my partner for comfort.

"Well," she said, "this is your orientation. Get used to it."

And I thought, "We're up in this helicopter with the full responsibility for patient care. There's no doctor and no one else around to help us make decisions. I hope I can do this."

Our patient died two days later. It was a hard introduction to my job. Yet despite the traumas I witness, I've learned to love the work I do. But it's certainly not for the weak or faint-hearted.

There's nothing worse than picking up a sick or injured person, busting your gut to make sure he or she survives, then having them suddenly die on you. It's like being on an emotional roller coaster for twelve hours a day.

I used to have trouble sleeping at night, second-guessing myself constantly about a call I had

The BK117 is one of the more common aircraft used in today's air rescue missions. Sturdily built and reliable, it is considered a workhorse within the air ambulance industry. (Kenny Jones, EMT/P, Hermann Life Flight/Houston, Texas)

Between flights MAMA—Mission Air Medical Ambulance—rests on the helopad in Asheville, North Carolina. (Mike Maher, 1992)

Paramedics and flight nurses often act as the pilot's extra pair of eyes and ears. Space is limited in the well-designed, but tight, interior. (Mike Maher, 1992)

Typically air ambulances have one-to-three–patient capacity. This North Carolina aircraft can carry only one patient at a time. (Mike Maher, 1992)

This dispatch communications center in Houston, Texas, serves as the vital link between Life Flight air ambulances and the hospital, monitoring flights and requests for service. (Kenny Jones, EMT/P, Hermann Life Flight/Houston, Texas)

MAMA's pilot makes a difficult approach through dense woods and rocky terrain during this river rescue in Asheville, North Carolina. (Virgil Bodenhamer, 1992)

The MAMA aircraft perches precariously on a flat rock upriver from the rescue scene as the crew prepares to make its way to the patient. (Virgil Bodenhamer, 1992)

Boaters strap their kayaks together to create a makeshift stretcher for Slim. (Virgil Bodenhamer, 1992)

The kayakers, along with paramedic Rieley Bennett from the MAMA crew, form a relay to transport Slim to the waiting helicopter. (Virgil Bodenhamer, 1992)

Air ambulance services are often called to the scene of major highway accidents. Here, the Hermann Life Flight teams work in tandem at the scene of a multiple car collision. (Kenny Jones, EMT/P, Hermann Life Flight/ Houston, Texas)

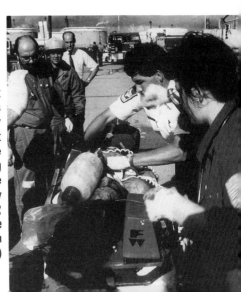

The Life Flight team stabilizes their seriously injured patient before transporting him to the hospital. (Kenny Jones, EMT/P, Hermann Life Flight/Houston Texas)

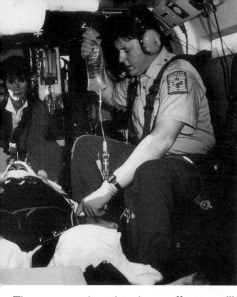

Intensive care continues during the flight. (Kenny Jones, EMT/P, Hermann Life Flight/Houston, Texas)

The race against time is an effort to utilize the "Golden Hour"—those critical sixty minutes after an accident or illness when treatment can often mean the difference between life and death. (Kenny Jones, EMT/P, Hermann Life Flight/Houston, Texas)

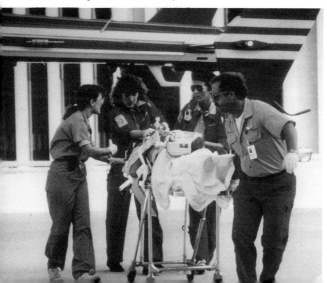

Rieley Bennett, paramedic with the MAMA crew in Asheville, North Carolina. (Mike Maher, 1992)

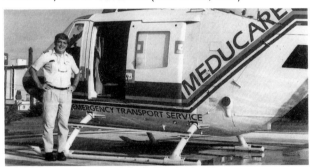

Pilot David Andrews, with the MEDUCARE team in Charleston, South Carolina. (Mike Maher, 1992)

Between flights, the MEDUCARE crew members wait, swapping stories and comparing notes, until the next emergency call comes in. (Mike Maher, 1992)

taken—what could I have done differently or better to benefit the patient?

But as you become more accustomed to the work, you learn there's only so much you can do.

A twenty-six-year-old engineer was on his way to work one morning on rain-slicked roads. The car flipped over and he landed fifty feet from the vehicle.

I had a nurse in training with me, and together we decided to load him on the helicopter and get him back to the hospital rather than try to treat him at the scene.

He was talking to me the entire time, and I was holding his hand. Just as we were landing at the hospital, he looked up at me and said, "Don't let me die. Please don't let me die."

I know when a patient has a sense of impending doom, something is about to happen. We unloaded him with the engines still running, but by the time we got him to the emergency room door, his heart stopped beating.

We did CPR, opened up his chest, performed every procedure we could, but he had torn the aorta, and there was nothing we could do to save him.

Both my partner and I walked into my office, sat down, and cried. The chief flight nurse tried to console us by telling us that even if we had an operating room on board the helicopter, we could not have saved this man.

Then his wife walks in, carrying a toddler, and she's obviously pregnant. She said they had just moved here, had no friends or relatives nearby.

That's the kind of thing that gets to you, and you think, "Why? Why did this have to happen?"

It is not only patients who take a toll on flight crew members, but the family and friends of victims:

People know that if their family member has been airlifted in, they can expect bad news, because we're equated with the most horrible things imaginable. It usually means someone has been scraped off the pavement or picked up in critical condition.

Yet those same people think that once we get to the hospital, everything is going to be all right. We have to deal with that a lot. And it's tough, because you don't always know what to say, or how to handle the situation.

Family members have watched me do cardiopulmonary resuscitation on a patient, and when the doctor comes to pronounce the person dead, they can't understand how my working on him didn't save him. How do you respond to that?

The truth is, we can't save everyone. But that's not what they want to hear.

This flight nurse was almost overwhelmed with the tragedy he encountered during a single twelve-hour shift:

It was my first summer flying, working nights, and I had only been on the job a few months.

We were called to the scene of an accident on the Gulf Freeway. When we arrived, the doctor and I went over to our patient, a fourteen-monthold child, who was sitting in the highway screaming her lungs out. She had a bad scalp laceration, so we tried to start an IV, but couldn't, and decided instead to load her onto the helicopter and get her back to the hospital as quickly as possible.

The pilot came over to help us put the child onto the stretcher, and as we headed back to the aircraft with her, he kept saying, "Watch where you step. Be careful. Watch out."

I looked down, thinking, "What is all this stuff?" Then it hit me. It was the body parts of dead victims.

The car was going northbound, lost control, became airborne, and hit the southbound side of the freeway, ripping the roof off the vehicle. Both occupants were killed instantly.

Another car, carrying two couples and a baby, was struck. All four adults were killed, but the baby, strapped in a car seat, survived. This was the child we were carrying.

It bothered me: Here were two young couples doing what they were supposed to be doing, and now here was a child with no parents.

Shortly after returning to the hospital that same night, I got called to a scene where a rock group was giving a private concert.

There was a hayride as part of the festivities, and during the ride, two young adults fell off the back of the wagon, which then rolled backwards onto them. The female victim was talking to us when we arrived. But she had massive pelvic injuries, and we soon lost her.

The male victim, not as seriously injured, was transported by air to the hospital. Both families had been notified and were waiting for us when we got there.

The girl's family expected to see her with us. I had to tell them she didn't make it and her body was coming by ambulance. She was a single parent, they said, leaving two small children behind. It was difficult dealing with their pain.

As I was talking to the family, my beeper went off and I got a call to respond to a twenty-one-year-old head injury patient. By now, I was physically and mentally exhausted.

On my way to the helicopter, I passed an emergency room nurse who took one look at me and said,, "Are you okay?"

I burst into tears.

"I don't think I can do this anymore," I cried. She gave me a hug and went on her way.

Another flight nurse came around the corner, and I stopped to ask her if she would consider taking my scene call.

"No," she said. "It's your call. You need to take your own flights."

At first I thought, "God, this is unbelievable. How cold can you get?"

But I learned two things: (1) I'd better get my act together, because in seven minutes I would be in another emergency room with another patient, and (2) I'd better learn to control my feelings about the job, or the job would control me.

Later, when I returned from my final call, that same nurse pulled me aside and said, "I hope you don't think I was being mean. But maybe now you understand what it takes to be a flight nurse. You're going to have tough cases and tough nights like this again. The sooner you accept it, the better off you—and your patients—will be."

It also made me realize that we can help each

other out, but only to a point. Whether or not I make it in this job is really up to me.

In this case, the flight nurse lost her cool in the middle of a rescue scene, one of her colleagues tells us:

She got frustrated and threw a piece of medical equipment at an ambulance crew member. Then she walked off the job. It made us angry, but we knew it was stress-related. She had not yet learned how to cope with the things that go wrong, and the patients that die.

After five years in the business, this Texas flight nurse says she is ready for a change of pace:

I've seen a lot of death and despair, and there are times when I can't take another call. On certain days, when I leave here, I want to go to work in a well-baby clinic—somewhere that people aren't dying.

The longer I'm in it, the more it wears on me. I feel like the "Black Widow."

I've found that flight nurses and paramedics either leave this job quickly, like within the first year; or they stay till they can't do it anymore. Either way, they never forget what they saw.

All flight members deal with the stress in their own private way, finding a defense system that works best for them:

A lot of people see us as cold and unfeeling, but we're not. In many circumstances, putting some distance between us and the patient or family is the only way we can cope.

I don't run up to meet every family member of a patient I've flown, for example, because if it's a bad outcome and I've established a link with that family, it's more than I can handle, especially on an everyday basis.

So keeping a certain distance is my defense mechanism.

After a while, the names and faces all start to blend together. And you think, "How can that be?"

I guess it's a defense mechanism, because it's hard to go home and dwell on it constantly—the blood, the guts, the trauma.

Plus it gives you a real perspective. People walk around saying they've had a bad day. But a bad day is when you get your legs caught under the wheel of a car at an accident site, or lose an arm, or have your child burned beyond recognition. It's *not* spilling coffee on your shirt.

You lock into the fact that you're doing a job, and you think you're removed from the pain. Then you meet the family, or something triggers a personal response.

I remember a scene that involved a law enforcement officer pinned under a truck. We finally got him out, but he was already dead.

As we rolled him over to prepare him for the ride to the morgue, a photo fell out of his wallet. It was a picture of a little girl, and across the top she had written, "I love you, Daddy."

I kept staring at it, thinking about all our skills and how none of them could save this officer.

Then I put the photo in his pocket and walked away. There was nothing more I could do.

Knowing when to walk away, head for time out, is one of the most valuable coping skills a flight nurse or paramedic can have:

This was a childbirth scene, one of the few times in the business when you kick back and say, "Great, we're gonna go and assist God and nature in a natural, joyous event."

It was the middle of the night when we got there, and I learned the child had been delivered at only five months' gestation. I walked in the room and saw this purple fetus that had no business being in the world yet, struggling to survive.

Unfortunately, we are not geared medically to deal with preemies that small. So I did the most basic procedure I could do, feeling helpless the entire time. Meanwhile, this tiny life was depending on me to pull it through.

As soon as we returned to the hospital, I turned the baby over to the emergency room staff, curled up on a bench, and just lay there, wondering if I'd be able to come back to work tomorrow. I didn't realize it at the time, but I had reached the point where I was totally stressed out.

I knew then I'd be going home early that night, and if anyone asked me why, I'd tell them I was temporarily out of service.

\* \* \*

There's an attitude among a lot of flight personnel like, "Hey, I'm tough. I can take it."

But they don't understand how vulnerable they
are day in and day out. Those are the ones who
get into trouble.

It's much healthier to say, "I've got to get off
this rig. I'm stressed out. I gotta go home."

In my case, I know when I'm on overload, and
I've learned to step back and do something about
it before it's too late.

It's not only the trauma of a scene call that few
people understand, but the day-to-day details of the
job. . . .

People see us in these uniforms, watch us ride
the helicopter, and think it's a lot of fun, but they
don't know what it's like to be out there in ninety-
eight-degree weather trying to wipe blood out of
the aircraft, or fly back-to-back scene calls in freezing temperatures with no breakfast or lunch.

When we're not flying, there are lots of mundane things that must be done, protocols to follow, reports to write, follow-ups to do, that can
be boring as hell.

A lot of people think we're trauma junkies,
and most of us do like the excitement, but the
truth is, when I'm working at a scene, I hardly
see anyone or anything around me.

My mind is going ninety miles an hour, trying
to remember everything I have to do, and making
sure I do it right.

I've worked in areas I've considered a war
zone—places where you have to look over your

shoulder while working on the patient to make certain no one is coming up behind you with a gun. Once I'm involved with the patient, however, I don't even let that bother me.

Once, I responded to a scene call in a bar downtown. While bent over the patient, I noticed a guy standing next to me with a machine gun strapped to his pants leg. Even I couldn't help but notice that. But I didn't even look up, just kept working with the patient. Later, I found out the guy was a policeman.

My point is, to me, this is more like a job, something you do by rote. That's my way of handling any stress and strain that goes with it.''

Despite their best efforts, most flight team members cannot avoid having their job spill over into their personal lives. After a particularly bad scene call, for example, or a day full of frustration, switching gears from flight nurse or paramedic to husband, wife, mother, or father is difficult at best. Certain types of situations flight teams encounter tap into their own anxieties about personal safety and the welfare of family members at home:

Kids go down the road beside our helicopter base each day—speeding, standing up in the back of an open vehicle.

We set our watches by them, knowing that in a few minutes or hours, someone will be calling us to rescue them from an accident. It makes those of us who have children worry.

Those of us who don't have children call these kids our ''job security.''

\* \* \*

As a mother, every time I hear the tones go off, indicating a scene call, I think it could be my child. And because it could happen, it has actually improved my relationship with my daughter.

Being on a scene is one thing, but if it involves one of your own, you wonder if you could deal with it, be the professional person everyone expects you to be.

One of the paramedics I worked with on a flight picked up a patient with facial injuries. No one recognized him until they got him to the hospital and the paramedic ran into his own family in the hallway.

It turned out the patient was his cousin and he didn't even know it.

Those are the kinds of things you fear the most.

My sister knows something horrible happened on the job when I call her and tell her, "Don't let the kids play on the swings anymore." I see what happens to children and I get overprotective. It drives her nuts.

With adult patients, it's easier to disassociate yourself from them because in a lot of cases, they're at fault. They've contributed to their accident, especially when it involves alcohol or drugs. But children are innocent victims.

There was a teenage couple at a prom who had been drinking, and were told by their parents not to drive. So they did the right thing and called for a ride.

The girl's uncle came to pick them up, but he was drinking, too. On the way home, he had an accident and killed the kids.

98

Even though he was my patient, I had a hard time being civil to him.

My kids say they hate it since I took this job. They can't have a four-wheeler, can't go out the door without my warnings about their being careful.

My sixteen-year-old daughter just totaled her car and wasn't wearing a seat belt at the time. I had an absolute fit. How many times do I have to tell her I don't want her as a patient?

I tend to worry about my own safety more, now than I've seen what can happen anywhere, anytime. There are certain things I especially fear. I don't want to be burned up in a house fire, or have a head injury, or be pinned in a car.

I don't tend to worry about crashing while we're flying. But I do worry about my daughter driving four hours to the beach and getting there all right.

It comes from seeing too many people in the wrong place at the wrong time.

Sometimes I do take the job home with me. I'll get there at midnight after having gone to a scene involving dead or injured children, and I'll go in my daughter's room, pick her up, and cry.

People often asked what type of individual enters this line of work. Who would willingly work with dead or dying patients? Why put themselves through that? And what is it that keeps them so involved?

This flight nurse says it's all about attitude:

You have to be a certain personality type to make it in this business—cocky, confident, sure of yourself. A strong ego helps, and the ability to make do with what you've got at the scene. If there aren't any neat little alcohol pads to sterilize a patient's wound, you improvise. And you'd better be able to make a decision, one way or the other. He who hesitates can kill.

Veteran flight nurses are more inclined to say they are in it for the challenge, especially when an unusual case presents itself:

For a lot of flight members, scene calls are the most exciting part of the work. And the media loves it when there's a dramatic rescue they can show on the six o'clock news.

But to me, any type of case that involves some creative thinking is a lot more interesting.

We went to a hospital to transport a patient who was in her early twenties, diagnosed with cancer of the throat. I expected to find her in the intensive care unit, but she was on the medical floor, sitting up on a hospital bed, looking perfectly normal.

The only thing unusual about her was that when she bent her head a certain way, she couldn't breathe. There was a huge mass obstructing her throat, and her doctors had decided she needed to be flown elsewhere for consultation.

My partner and I knew she was not going to survive the flight without being intubated. But the hospital crew—everyone from the doctor to the anesthetist—had already said they didn't feel comfortable putting a tube down her throat.

So this was turning into a serious dilemma.

It was not a black-and-white scene call, where you know what you have to do going in, and you do it. Instead, this patient had elected to be transported. But there was no easy way to get that accomplished safely.

I looked at my partner and he looked at me as if to say, "We're going to intubate, right?" "Right." "Right?"

Each was seeking reassurance, waiting for a nod from the other.

We plunged ahead, giving her a sedative that almost knocked her out so we could get the tube in her throat.

It was a nerve-racking experience. The larynx and trachea funneled down to nothing because of the mass, which produced extensive swelling.

When we finally got the tube in, it was like, "Whew! I'm glad that's over! Let's get out of here."

We flew her back to our hospital and brought her into the emergency room. But to them, there was no high drama in this case. It wasn't a scene call. It was just another medical patient—no bleeding, no cardiac arrest, more of a "So what?"


There is a love-hate relationship that often exists between hospitals and the flight teams they employ. Much of the relationship is colored and shaped by attitudes of both parties—whether or not hospital administrators see the flight program as a viable operation, for example, or how the helicopter flight team presents itself to hospital staff.

Once a flight program is well established, however, and the general public begins to expect the service it provides, both the hospital and flight operation become dependent on each other.

But this doesn't always mean that attitudes will change:

When our program first began, hospital administrators treated us like we were nothing more than emergency room nurses put on a helicopter. They cautioned us against thinking we were anything "special."

But we're in a different environment than anyone in the emergency room. Our job requires different skills and different thought processes. And we wish they understood that.

We brought a patient [without any life signs] into the emergency room one time, and the cardiovascular surgeon looked at him and said, "Why did you bring this guy in? You should have pronounced him dead at the scene."

I thought that was really out of line. After all, our job was to bring the patient to the place where he could get the best possible care. The paramedic with me was so disgusted, he just turned around and walked out.

We still get the attitude from the emergency room staff that if we're not out flying, we're not really working. And if it gets busy in the ER and we're not there to help, believe me, we hear about it and know there's going to be some resentment.

There was a lot of animosity between us and other nurses in the hospital when we started out—jealousy, resentment that we got the glory and they got the work.

Other nurses see us as "top of the heap," something they strive to be. I know there are people out there who want my job.

Some nurses and physicians think highly of you, while others think you're nothing more than a glorified transport team.

You'll bring the patient in after flying in 110-degree heat, lifting heavy stretchers, doing everything you can to stabilize this patient, and they'll say, "How come you didn't put the patient on a monitor?"

Or they'll make a sarcastic remark.

"I see you didn't get the glass out of his hair," said one emergency room nurse.

"I was a little busy," I responded. "I was trying to *get the car off his body*."

Inadvertently, patients can be the cause of relationship problems between the flight team and hospital nurses:

The patient comes to us and says, "Thank you, you saved my life," when, in reality, we were only with him a few minutes.

They never think to appreciate the nurse who worked her tail off for two weeks after we got him to the hospital.

It inevitably sets up a certain amount of resentment.

This paramedic takes a down-to-earth approach that he says has prevented a lot of hostility on the job:

Everyone thinks we are so elite. But I don't think so. We're a tough bunch, but we're no different than any other health care professional. Any nurse could do this job.

Other flight team members carry a certain amount of resentment toward their employers, who, they say, simply don't appreciate what they're about:

We're the redheaded stepchild to our administration. When we're out of sight, we're out of mind. People in the hospital don't even know who we are sometimes. We've been mistaken for everything from the maintenance crew to a NASA team visiting the hospital.

However, the media thinks we are gold. They'll turn up at a scene with their cameras before we even get there.

Unfortunately, they never get our names right.

It is with the media that flight teams know exactly where they stand:

The media can make you look like this wonderful hero, or the world's biggest fool. They decide whether to show you saving a life or pulling up your underwear.

So it pays to earn their friendship.

Not surprisingly, considering the experiences they share, there is a special kind of bond that develops among the flight crew members. As a whole, they tend to work as a tightly knit team. Within that team are partners—flight nurse and paramedic, along with whichever pilot is on call—who work together as a unit on each helicopter flight. The relationships that emerge from these units are similar to the partnerships found between cops, who routinely place their lives in each other's hands:

This is a business in which you learn to appreciate your partner, and trust that person completely, because so much depends on the two of you, both medically and in the air.

The bonding begins when you're in the helicopter sharing experiences. It's like going into combat for the first time. Each new person has to prove himself.

For example, you can be sitting on one side of the helicopter daydreaming instead of serving as an extra pair of eyes for the crew. You miss seeing a wire, we drive into it, and within the next instant, you've helped kill everyone on board, including yourself.

Or you let down your defenses in a bad situation and you're as stressed out as you can be, letting your coworkers see you at your worst.

That's why so many of us become so close.

My partner and I went to Chattanooga, Tennessee, and got trapped by bad weather. We spent the night at the hospital. The next day, conditions didn't look any better, so we were stuck again. The hospital was really nice to us, gave us scrub suits and a place to sleep.

I called our boss and told him he could either pay us all this overtime, or send us a plane ticket home. He sent the tickets.

We have a certain amount of narcotics we have to carry at all times, for which we are held accountable.

So here we were at the airport, dressed in scrub suits, carrying a tote bag of drugs, and trying to get through security.

What really made it embarrassing was that after they checked us out, they made us board before everyone else, even the ones needing assistance.

We talked about that for days.

We take patients into San Francisco a lot, even though the city has an ordinance against helicopter pads. So we either land by the pier, the waterfront, or at Christy Field. We usually get an ambulance to pick us up, but they don't like waiting for us.

As a result, my partner and I once got stranded with no way back to our home base. We had all our gear, including a stretcher, which my partner strapped to his back. Here we are at two in the morning, walking up and down San Francisco streets looking for a cab. Try getting a cab with a stretcher strapped on your back!

We finally got a ride, but we were not happy campers.

\*   \*   \*

Overall, our flight team is a tight group. We see more of each other than we do of our families.

And it's amazing what we share and talk about. It's like having a whole lot of brothers and sisters.

The flip side of that closeness is the same as in any family—especially among "brother and sisters: Too much togetherness mean sparks are bound to fly. . . .

We can go somewhere as a team, get into a disagreement, and people think we hate each other. That's not true at all.

We're intense, type A personalities. Otherwise, we wouldn't be in this business. So it's inevitable, working closely together over long periods of time, that we'll butt heads.

But we always work it out, away from the patient and the families.

We've all had our arguments, our peaks and valleys as a team. But when I'm on a flight, it's not "you nurse," or "you paramedic." It's "partner" or "team member."

And when I need support or help with a problem, I know where to turn. Who else but my colleagues would understand?

Historically, such egalitarian attitudes have been lacking in the medical profession. Even now there are few women paramedics (most say they can make more money in nursing) and even fewer female pilots.

Flight nurses, however, are a different story. Statistically, there are more female flight nurses than males, and it is the men who are still trying to establish their identity in nursing.

People still assume, say flight crew members, that any male in a uniform is a pilot. Within the team itself, the issue is not one of sexism, but of power and rank:

Paramedics have to learn to deal with opinionated, strong-willed nurses. Most paramedics have come from ambulance crews where they were in charge and made their own decisions.

As a member of the flight team, paramedics complain that *nurses* always want to be in charge.

One paramedic told me his definition of an R.N. is "someone who likes to boss people around."

Women in this business tend to be very aggressive, very independent, and constantly striving to improve themselves. We're also very competitive. Some men can't deal with that.

I meet a lot of men who are intimidated when they find out I'm a flight nurse, especially when we talk salaries.

They think I'm "Miss Moneybags."

Everyone, in fact, assumes we make more than regular nurses, but we don't.

Yet power and rank take a backseat position when men and women, working close together, let nature take its course:

Yeah, there's some flirting that goes on, too. Affairs happen, usually between pilots and nurses, but they are frowned upon by supervisors. Whether or not you get away with it depends upon how much pull you have.

Anyway, it's hard to keep a secret because we work in such close proximity. You can be in a different room, even think about having an affair, and before long, the whole team will know about it. Everybody knows everybody else's business.

We went out to the airport one night and opened the door to the fixed wing office. There was one of our pilots and one of our nurses in a compromising situation.

They were so shocked and embarrassed to be caught, they both put in for a transfer. They are now married.

It's interesting to watch a couple who are involved while on the job, because they treat each other differently. You can actually see the relationship evolve, running its entire course, in and out of stressful conditions.

Stress is at its highest when a helicopter nurse or paramedic screws up, makes a mistake on the job that affects a patient's status. It is during this time that a colleague's support—or lack of it—can make or break a working relationship:

If you screw up, you'd better make it known to your partner, or you'll both be nailed.

You don't have to make a big mistake in this job for there to be serious consequences. It could simply be a matter of not doing something as well as you should have.

It's always a learning experience. But I can guarantee one thing. If you do screw up major, you don't usually get another chance.

In this flight nurse's case, the patient would have died as a result of her error:

We had been doing cardiopulmonary resuscitation on this patient for about an hour before I realized I had placed the tube that allows him to breathe into his esophagus instead of his trachea. However, his stomach filled with so much air, it sounded like he was okay, so I thought the procedure was done properly.

We brought him into the trauma unit—still doing CPR on him—and just as luck would have it, my head nurse is on duty that day and receives him as her patient.

She kept saying, "This isn't right. This isn't right."

Even after several doctors checked him and said, "Yeah, he appears to be intubated," she kept persisting. And she was correct.

I explained my part in it, and she agreed that if the patient had not already been dead, I would have killed him.

I fucked up. I really did. It's something I learned from, will never do again, and will never stop kicking myself in the ass for. But a lot of people are safer now because I admitted it, dealt with it, and learned from it.

\* \* \*

You're expected to think and work under extremely trying conditions, and be right all of the time. I can see why some nurses and paramedics quit.

But no one is more critical of us than we are of ourselves.

You can cover up a lot, especially if you know your patient is going to die anyway. But we all have to live with what we do.

Because of that, you will second-guess yourself from here to eternity. Why didn't I do this? Or what could I have done differently?

Then you finally realize: You're just a nurse. A good one, but human like everyone else.

When people say things like "Angels have descended," referring to us, I don't deal with that well.

We're just like everyone else. We have our good days and our bad. And we don't know everything.

I also hate it when pilots say, "Oh, our team knows as much as any doctor." That's nonsense.

If you watch me close enough, I will screw up.

Our flight program doesn't offer a lot of support when you make a mistake. There's a feeling here that no one is supposed to screw up. And when you do, it's not discussed.

I have a friend who's also a flight nurse, who was assigned to go on a flight with a baby. Unless you come from pediatrics, you don't know that everything is done differently with a child. She had already experienced

111

having a child die in her care, so she was nervous to start with.

There was no doctor available to go with her, and she didn't want to go. But you can't say that. You'll be fired if you say you're afraid to make a flight. She called our boss to discuss the situation and was told, "You either be on that flight or be in my office at seven in the morning."

She took the flight, but a few days later, called and said she was thinking of quitting her job. It was obvious she had reached her limit of stress.

She told me about another flight that occurred a few days before. The patient had shot himself in the head with a .357 Magnum, and his vital signs were so bad when the helicopter got there, it was obvious he was dying.

"But I forgot to put oxygen into the bag," she said. "He couldn't breathe."

"Don't even sweat that stuff," I told her. "Put it behind you. Just don't ever do it again."

The sad part is, most people in our program won't admit to making a mistake, so there's nowhere to turn for help. And I think that's wrong.

I know I'm human. And I'll admit it to anyone.


For every error in judgment that occurs, there are literally thousands of procedures handled properly, skills well utilized, decisions made wisely, lives saved that would otherwise be lost.

Flight crews refer to these as "good calls"—the

ones in which patients realize that without the helicopter crew, they would not be alive to express their thanks:

We were dispatched one night to the Bay area on the West Coast, landing in the parking lot of a realty office. From there, we were driven by fire truck to a yacht club where an elderly gentleman had collapsed and was in cardiac arrest.

When we arrived, he had already been unconscious (and not breathing) for what we thought was longer than survival time.

We were in an area where we couldn't make contact with our hospital to ask for instruction, so my partner and I decided to proceed on our own. We have provisions and the equipment that allows us to bypass protocol.

We began CPR, and lo and behold, ten minutes later our patient comes back with a pulse. By the time we loaded him onto the helicopter, he was trying to talk. A week later he left the hospital.

Every so often, he stops by the fire department where we treated him and says, "Thanks a lot, guys. You saved my life."

It was a real shot in the arm for us, because there had been some controversy about whether or not our services were really needed.

Even more important, we felt like our high-tech equipment and advanced training made a difference.

To have someone appreciate you for doing what you're supposed to do, be genuinely grate-

ful, and give you a pat on the back is a real
morale boost.

It made us feel our services were truly
important.

Being applauded for their efforts, and believing in
themselves, is what keeps the helicopter flight teams
striving for perfection. And knowing they will never
reach that goal—but continuing to try—is what makes
their struggle heroic:

Within the first ten minutes after a case, we'll
be asking ourselves, "Did I do everything I
could? Or should I have tried something different? Would that have changed the outcome?"

Ninety-nine percent of the time, there's nothing we could have done any better.

It's tough, tragic, to see what we see—people
torn all to hell, sometimes by their own stupid
actions.

But there's no better technology in prehospital
care than a helicopter and a good flight team.

People are still going to die. But then some
won't.

And I believe it's because we give them our
best shot.

# 6
# *Politics & Perspectives*

*"When we get off that helicopter and two or three ambulance ground crews are there, we know we have to kiss their butts. And we do it—for the ultimate welfare of the patient."*

—Flight paramedic

HUMAN NATURE BEING WHAT IT IS, THERE IS A CERtain amount of conflict that is bound to arise when a large number of people, all of whom play important roles, are forced to work together for a common good. Strong egos inevitably clash, differences of opinion arise, jealousies and resentments surface. Territorialism and an outta-my-face attitude emerge. It is collective team spirit gone bad, the darker side of otherwise perfectly decent human beings.

It is also politics, pure and simple, and it is alive and well in emergency medical service, as this male flight nurse found out:

> I was on a scene call where there were dozens of people around, the media was there, and the gawkers were there with their video cameras.
>
> The victim's face was torn up and she desper-

115

Marie Bartlett Maher

ately needed an airway. But the emergency medical technician from the ambulance crew was just standing there, doing nothing.

So I walked over, took the instrument out of his hand, and started working on the patient. By the time we got back to the hospital, it had already been reported as a major "incident."

It was a public relations and interagency problem until they looked at the video to see exactly what I'd done.

Maybe I was out of line, but that's just the way I am. And I know it will happen again.

Indeed, it probably will, for there remains an uneasy alliance between all too many medical flight programs and the ground crews with whom they must work, and with whom they compete for patients.

"Before we make a flight," said a North Carolina helicopter medical director, "we have to feel each county out and determine what their politics are. On one end of the spectrum, you have emergency medical service directors who give their ground crew paramedics full authority, upon examination of the patient, to call us directly to the scene. It's a given that they want us to transport the patient back to our home hospital.

"On the other end of the spectrum, there are counties where ground crew paramedics are told to *never* call the helicopter, no matter what the patient's condition. They are instructed, instead, to take the patient to *their* home hospital, where the medical director, upon making an examination, determines where that patient will go."

This same flight crew supervisor says that when his

program first got under way six years ago, ground crew paramedics in one rural county had to meet with their supervisor and justify their action each time they called the helicopter crew. As a result, the ambulance personnel in that county refused to contact the flight team even when it would have meant faster transport for the patient, because they didn't want the frequent meetings with their boss that would automatically follow.

In some instances, territorialism is the issue.

"It's a matter of 'This is my space and you're coming into it,' " says a North Carolina chief flight nurse.

Even more important, from the hospital's point of view, it's a matter of economic survival. When a patient is transported by ambulance to a local county hospital, that facility gets the revenue generated by that particular patient. When a helicopter crew comes in and whisks the patient back to *their* home hospital, it's like taking money out of the local facility's pocket.

But there are egos involved, too, in the tug-of-war for patients.

In one rural state, the relationship between "the air guys" and "the ground guys" became so strained, ambulance personnel set out to prove they could transport patients quicker than the helicopter could.

"It became a race against the clock," recalls one flight paramedic. "They would call us to the scene, we'd get the patient, then they would book it back to the emergency room, timing themselves to see if they could 'beat' us. The idiocy was that in an effort to make their point, they sped ninety miles an hour and ran red lights, endangering the general public."

Ironically, he added, the "race" had one hidden benefit.

"Since our program was new and we were not yet familiar with outlying areas, it gave us a reading on where we actually saved time by flying to the scene, and where we didn't."

Yet all emergency medical teams agree that when "ground guys" and "air guys" spend too much time focusing on how they can outdo each other, it is the patient who winds up suffering the most.

"In our state," says a flight program medical director, "when we started out, we had to go to great lengths not to make anyone mad. If we did, the response was, 'To hell with the patient. I'm not going to call the flight team.' That's when everyone forgets what's important in this whole scenario—the patient. If everybody would ask, 'What's best for the patient?' then politics would be gone. But you've got politics in the administration of emergency medical services, among air and ground crews, and in hospitals. Everyone wants their piece of the pie from patient revenue."

This same director says that as the helicopter flight team became better established, it was perceived as less of a threat, and more of an adjunct service to overall emergency medicine.

"Hospitals and ground crew services saw we weren't going to swoop down and take their patients away unless all the criteria [for airlift transport] were met," he says. "That's when they began to accept us."

With acceptance, however, comes responsibility from all the parties involved, to keep the problems at bay. That's where helicopter flight crews are accountable for sometimes adding fuel to the fire. This is what a chief flight nurse in the South, known for his sense of fair play, has to say:

"All you need is one flight crew member strutting in with the mirrored shades on, pushing the ground crew paramedic out of the way, saying, 'Give me your patient,' and you've done a world of damage."

Even more revealing is a side of the story told from the emergency ground crew's perspective:

"In the beginning," says a former ground paramedic, "emergency service personnel in outlying areas saw the helicopter program as a godsend. Our state's paramedic program was only two years old at the time, and we were trying to get our feet on the ground. Then we saw how pushy the helicopter flight crew really was. The flight team would sit around and monitor the scanner, listening for reports of an accident, and when they heard something that sounded 'interesting,' they would immediately depart on what they called a 'training flight.' Then they would hover over the scene, calling down to us, 'Need any help?' It was very annoying. In one incident, we had a wreck with a person trapped inside the car, and the helicopter was making so much noise above us, we couldn't even communicate with each other!

"The irony was that their landing time and our ground transport time wasn't that much different, so we didn't think they had that much more to offer the patient, other than the 'hoopla' that surrounds every flight."

He says his real concern was that the helicopter

was "fooling around" at a scene unnecessarily when it may have been needed more urgently elsewhere.

"I saw it as a misuse of resources," he says.

In addition, he says, the hospital where the flight team originated shares the blame.

"The hospital had this expensive flight program, and they wanted numbers to justify the cost. That meant getting the helicopter out there—see and be seen—transporting patients who didn't always need to have that extra seven hundred dollars added to their bill, compared to ninety dollars if they were transported by ambulance."

Since then, he adds, his region's flight team and ground crew teams have ironed out many of their initial problems and are working together on a much more professional level.

But there are still ground crew personnel who feel threatened by what they see as a "takeover" by flight crews, others who use the helicopter as a "crutch"—calling them to a scene because they don't feel good about their own skills—and a third group who have come to terms with the flight team's role and see it as just another facet of emergency medical service.

Despite their best intentions, helicopter flight programs are not always warmly received by local communities either.

In California, residents housed near the hospital where a helicopter program was based were so upset by the noise the helicopter created during patient flights, they wrote letters of protest to newspaper editors and formed a small but powerful neighborhood coalition that nearly crippled the hospital's program.

One neighbor complained to the city council that

the helicopter "sounds like it's coming through my window to land on the carpet by my bed." Other hospital neighbors said the flights were potentially dangerous, too near to their homes, and often unnecessary.

As a result, city government, responding to the neighborhood taxpayers, put pressure on the Catholic-owned hospital (located inside the city limits) to restrict emergency flights to a limited number per month, regardless of the number of requests for patient transport.

The quota set off a storm of protest, ending up in what the local media soon tagged "the chopper wars."

Specifically, the neighborhood wanted to reduce the flights to five a month, even after the flights were restricted to twelve. The hospital said no way. Many wanted the quota ended altogether.

"Curtailing the number of flights doesn't seem a fair way to pay respect to human life," said one local official.

"It's pretty damned frustrating to be at the scene with a critically injured man and not be able to airlift him because the helipad is closed," said the flight team's program director.

"With this quota system," said a fire captain who often called on the flight team for help, "someone is going to die on the highway or out on the coast."

Incidents did occur in which seriously ill or injured patients were refused airlift transport because the program had reached its limit for the month. In some cases, the hospital simply ignored the restrictions and flew the patient anyway.

As of 1992, after years of debate, the dispute remained unresolved. Helicopter flights were still limited to twelve per month, or thirty-six per quarter.

"The patient unfortunate enough to be number thirty-seven is just out of luck," said a local newspaper publisher.

Most flight team members say they had no idea when they entered the profession that medicine was such a political arena.

"I guess I was naive," says one paramedic. "I had delusions of grandeur that I was going to swoop down from the sky and heal people. After doing this for a year, however, I know now it's as important to stroke the physicians, the hospitals, and the public as it is to give good patient care. I've had to temper myself accordingly."

His colleagues, he says, are still learning that valuable lesson. . . .

Administrators don't always put the patient's best interests first. We went on a call to respond to a severely injured patient, and the doctor in charge of our program insisted we take a film crew along.

I said, "What are we here for—to make a movie or treat the patient?"

You go to the hospital administrator and tell him you need a new ventilator, and he'll say, "Can't you do it by hand?"

Or you'll ask for a new piece of equipment that will make your job a lot easier, and be told, "You've used it for four years. Can you make do for a bit longer?"

But they haven't been on a scene call, and don't understand that a particular piece of equipment could spell the difference between whether someone lives or dies.

The bottom line for them is always the cost.

Because of the politics of New York City, our flight program is not always well received. We are restricted, for example, to certain landing sites, and it appears at times that patient care is the last thing on anyone's mind.

We had a guy with a heart transplant going to a hospital, but getting him there turned into a major hassle.

I was attempting to find a place to land, and the dispatcher was saying, "Oh, you don't need to land here. Just go over to Sixtieth Street."

Meanwhile, our patient's blood pressure is dropping and he's going into cardiac arrest.

I said, "Wait a minute! Sixtieth Street is a hundred-and-twenty-block drive across the city!"

At the same instant, I'm getting clearance from the airport to land somewhere else, and now I don't know where the hell I'm supposed to go.

The patient was very lucky in that he lived long enough for us to finally get him to a hospital, but none of that should have happened.

It shouldn't be a race, and it shouldn't be a squabble over who can land where.

In this scene call, the territorial issue was settled by breaking the rules, but only after the patient suffered unnecessarily:

We were told to meet the ambulance at the scene. A huge propane tank had exploded at this guy's house and he was badly injured. Burns covered his entire body, but he was awake, and in a lot of pain.

Arrangements were quickly made to pick him up at one hospital and fly him to a burn center in Berkeley, California. But the center didn't have a helicopter pad, so instead, we were directed to land at a naval base hospital and take a ground ambulance to Berkeley.

I don't know how it happened, but when we landed at the naval hospital, the ambulance wasn't there to meet us.

A navy ambulance was available to get us from the helicopter pad to their hospital, but they had no intention of transporting us off the naval base to the burn center.

We sat in the back of the navy ambulance with our patient screaming in pain. One of his IV lines had clotted and was not running. And we were starting to get low on morphine because of the delay.

Finally a lieutenant commander stuck his head in the back of the ambulance.

I said, "Listen, man, you've got to do us a favor. This patient needs to be in the hospital, and I don't know where the hell our ambulance is. So please let your guys take us to the burn center. I will do whatever I have to do with the people above you to cover your butt. The way it is now, we're doing this man a great injustice by sitting here."

The lieutenant commander didn't say anything, left the scene, then returned a few minutes later.

"Do it," he said. "I'll get my ass chewed off, but do it anyway."

I still don't know what happened to our ambulance. Some kind of screw-up, I guess.

Most frustrating of all, the patient died two days later.

Working with doctors and hospitals in other areas outside their home base is often a delicate balancing act for flight crew members who must look out for their patient's best interests, while avoiding stepping on toes:

A lot of our job is public relations. It's shocking what we sometimes see in hospital care, but you can't go in and say, "Why the hell did you do that?"

Doctors, in particular, have a hard time giving up their patient to a nurse, when technically it's our patient once we're called to go in.

We have trouble sometimes with outlying hospitals in rural areas. This little lady was about eighty-seven years old and she had some kind of cardiac problem.

We had been called to transport her, and when we arrived we prepared to change her pacemaker cables to our portable unit. I started to unplug the hospital's cable set, and the doctor in charge, who was standing there, went into a fit.

I felt a lot of it was pure performance—him letting us know who was in charge.

We got her ready to go to the helicopter, and he said we should keep her on the hospital's unit by using a long extension cord rather than

125

applying a battery pack. It was going to take an awfully long extension cord to make it all the way to the helicopter.

That's how ridiculous it can get.

Even the patient's family couldn't believe his behavior.

Most doctors are really glad to see us. I've been asked to do things for a patient that would normally be considered in-house physician procedures. So I feel that we generally get the respect we deserve.

There are times, however, when mistakes are made—the hospital staff giving the patient wrong medication, or arguing with the flight crew to prove a point—and you have to let them know tactfully that you're there to do your job. The trick is to do it without alienating anyone.

If we had not been at the hospital, this particular patient would have died.

He was suffering from pulmonary edema, which means his lungs were filling up with fluid, and they had given him a medication to counteract that, but which can cause erratic heartbeat. His blood pressure was dangerously low when we arrived, and falling fast.

And he was still awake.

The doctor was leaning over him when we walked in, and the first thing this physician said to us was, "I don't want you to fly him out because he's going to die."

Our flight nurse responded, "Not if I can help it!"

We started prodding the doctor to do some of the things we felt would help, like giving the patient more oxygen and medication to reduce the pulmonary pressure.

The doctor went along with that, but then walked down the hall to our pilot and said, "No need to fly this man. He's going to die." He had a nurse with him, and she was fuming at what she considered our "interfering."

Normally, to avoid that kind of conflict, we would load him onto the stretcher, put him in the helicopter, and leave.

But this was a situation where we hadn't been told officially that the man was our patient.

The patient's lungs were still full of rattles, but after we medicated him, his chest pains lessened and we felt that at least he was getting oxygen.

The doctor returned to the room and spoke to the patient.

"You might die if you fly out of here," he said.

"I've made my decision," the man answered. "I want to go."

We put him on a stretcher and started down the hallway with him. The hospital nurse followed behind. At one point, I turned to her and apologized for being pushy.

"I don't think you're pushy," she said. "I think you're downright rude." Then she completely ignored us.

By the time we got him back to our hospital, his condition had improved dramatically. In fact, he was laughing and joking with us.

The next day, the nurse called my medical director to complain about me, denying that the doctor had even been in the room.

It's a very sensitive area, dealing with other hospitals and their staff, but you try to consider the patient first, then do what you think is best.

You learn to smile in this business, no matter what. You act professional and pleasant at all times, even when someone is pushing all your buttons. Then you get your patient out of there as quickly as possible, and undo any damage that was done.

Competing for patients can get down and dirty, as it did in this small town, where two helicopter flight programs are based within close proximity of each other:

We were grounded for routine maintenance, and our competitor across town called the media and told them we were having engine trouble, implying our flights were no longer safe.

They've also refused to transport patients for us because the truth is, we get more calls than they do.

We believe our program is safer and more patient-oriented than theirs, but we've had to take a lot of backstabbing while establishing our reputation.

This chief flight nurse, hip to the political manifestations of the job, says he understands there is little he can do to change things. But he also believes that nothing, not even politics, can devalue the human service that his crew provides:

I'm not naive enough to think that if the hospital got into dire straits financially, they wouldn't consider eliminating us. Because they would.

But I also realize what it is we offer—a solid public service that is going to continue to grow, one which people will come to know has real and lasting value.

# 7
# *Fear of Flying*

*"I never held another female's hand until we had a close call in a helicopter. No one has to say anything. It's a look or a smile that says—we made it."*

—Tennessee flight nurse

THERE ARE NURSES AND PARAMEDICS WHO LOVE THE unpredictability of emergency medicine, but hate the uncertainty of flying. Just the sheer act of leaving the ground can bring tremors to otherwise calm hands, turning normally composed individuals into white-knuckled, Valium-popping wrecks.

"It's one of the reasons I quit the helicopter program," says a former flight nurse, renowned for her cool, collected manner in emergency situations.

"Every time I knew we were going on a flight, I would get physically ill from sheer fright. I knew that didn't bode well for my patients, so I came back to the emergency room, where I can keep my feet on the ground."

Her colleagues in the hospital, where she is now a supervisor, agree that not everyone is cut out to be a flight nurse.

"The flight teams don't always believe this," says one hospital-based nurse, "but some of us don't want to be part of their group. While flying can be exciting, it's also an uncontrolled environment. The last time I went up on a public relations flight, it was a cold, windy day, and we had a lot of turbulence. It frightened me, made me glad I could return to the hospital, where I belong."

Even veteran flight team members have reservations about this aspect of nursing.

"When people tell me they want a job like mine," says a six-year flight paramedic, "my response is, 'When's the last time you had a better than average chance of getting killed giving someone a sponge bath?'"

There is cause for such trepidation.

Since 1972, when the first helicopter went on contract for a hospital as an alternative to ground ambulance transport, more than seventy helicopter crashes have occurred nationwide. By 1986, a particularly bad year for emergency medical service, with thirteen accidents, the industry had acquired a relatively poor safety record, leading to questions about the validity of air service versus ground transport.

One of those tragedies occurred on September 23, 1986, at a brand-new air flight program at Bowman Gray Hospital in Winston-Salem, North Carolina.

About 8:00 A.M. that day, a hospital in Galax, Virginia—forty-five minutes away by air—requested that the AirCare flight team pick up a patient for transfer. Weather delayed the flight until past noon, but once the aircraft took off, everything appeared normal.

On board was flight nurse Karen Simpson, thirty, and her best friend and coworker, Barbara Burdett, a fresh-faced novice, eager to learn the new job. Barbara had just celebrated her twenty-eighth birthday. The pilot was Barry Day, a Houston, Texas, native, thirty-six, with an easy grin and pleasant manner.

Shortly after departing Winston-Salem, Barry, known as an experienced, careful pilot, crossed the North Carolina–Virginia line, headed toward Galax.

Six minutes away from his expected time of arrival, Barry called the dispatcher to report his whereabouts. Thick fog had moved into the region, obstructing his vision, but for reasons that no one can determine, Barry chose not to turn back.

Instead, approaching Fisher Peak, a densely wooded region in Carroll County, Virginia, he circled the area, looking for a place to land. Unable to find a suitable site, he forged ahead, striking the peak just twenty feet below its summit.

Witnesses living near the crash site site said it sounded like the engine was pulling hard. Then there was a clicking noise, and the helicopter lunged toward the mountain. Moments later, there was a huge explosion. The impact killed everyone on board and set off two separate fires in the woods.

At AirCare headquarters in Winston-Salem, radio communicators were puzzled by the sudden loss of contact. A call to Galax produced no answers. North Carolina's Duke University's Life Flight helicopter, on a nonemergency mission in the same vicinity where the crash occurred, diverted to AirCare's last known position. Fifteen minutes later, they spotted the wreckage. It had cut a path through the woods nearly 350 yards long.

Analyzing the accident, the National Transportation Safety Board determined the probable cause was pilot error, specifically not maintaining proper altitude, plus rough terrain and foggy weather conditions.

It was a hard pill for the newly formed AirCare program to swallow, but they were determined to suffer their losses and go on. Efforts to locate replacement equipment and another helicopter began the next day.

"It was a very trying time," said Susan Butler, chief flight nurse for AirCare. "We were emotionally fragile for a while. But those of us left were committed to the program and didn't want it to end."

A year later, there were three more accidents across the country, and six more in 1989. Four of those six involved fatalities.

On January 26, 1991, a hospital helicopter had transferred a juvenile patient to another medical facility in Danville, Pennsylvania, and was returning to its home base when it clipped a stand of fifty-foot trees, slamming into a northern Pennsylvania mountain, about one hundred feet from its peak. Everyone aboard was killed instantly, including the pilot, a flight nurse, paramedic, and an emergency medical technician.

Snow was falling when the helicopter crashed, making weather a contributing factor. Pilot error was another. According to news reports, the aircraft was equipped to fly in cloudy weather, but it was uncertain whether or not the pilot had clearance to continue.

According to an aviation study conducted between 1972 and 1989, there are four leading causes of helicopter accidents: bad weather conditions, which account for about 29 percent of all accidents; obstacles such as bird strikes or power lines; engine failure; and control loss, which includes pilot error. In 1989, when six air medical accidents were recorded, four of which involved fatalities, pilot error was listed as the primary cause in 83 percent of the cases. Bad weather accounted for the remaining 17 percent.

Yet Mike Korn, an upstate New York mechanic who specializes in repairs and maintenance on all types of aircraft, says helicopters are much safer than most people think. He laughs when he hears the aircraft described as "a rock with an attitude."

"It's more like a hair dryer blowing on a pinwheel," he says. "But don't be fooled. These machines are built tough."

For every twenty-five hours "the bird" is in flight, Mike does a thorough examination, checking each component down to the last detail.

"I look at everything with a magnifying glass," he says. "And I make sure no one else tinkers with the aircraft."

Occasionally he flies with a pilot to make sure everything is in proper working order. The only bad experience he had was when the pilot—testing an engine by turning it off in midair—dropped the helicopter fifteen hundred feet in thirty seconds.

"I don't think I want to do *that* again," he says.

Compared to other aircraft, helicopters have few mechanical problems, says Mike.

"If you took the human factor out of it," he adds, "you'd have an almost flawless machine."

Improvements in safety and equipment standards, a shift toward the use of twin-engine as opposed to single-engine helicopters (44 percent of helicopters were twin-engine in 1985; the number rose to more than 70 percent in 1989), managerial emphasis on safety, and better-trained pilots have all contributed to a more safety-conscious environment within the air medical industry.

So has the move away from the "dash for cash" syndrome, in which flight teams feel pressured to go after revenue-producing patients even when weather conditions are marginal. Hospitals know there are times when it is better to turn patients down than unnecessarily risk the lives of crew and patient alike.

It is a clear sign that this relatively new form of patient transport, at least as an organized business, is finally coming of age.

Historically, the helicopter was invented for child's play. Its origin can be traced to China, where, more than two thousand years ago, someone invented a gyrocopter as a toy for children. Hundreds of years later, Leonardo da Vinci improved upon the design, though it still lacked a mechanical means to provide power. In 1754 a Russian scientist built a working model of an air screw, and a year later, two French experimenters managed to build a small helicopter theoretically capable of vertical flight.

However, it was 1907 before a helicopter became airborne. The flight took place in France, when the aircraft lifted itself and a pilot three feet off the ground.

Not long after, the military took an interest in helicopters—particularly the Germans, who put time and money into helicopter research and development in the 1930s, preparing for World War II. A few helicopters were used in wartime maneuvers, but it wasn't until the Korean War that the United States recognized their value for supply transport.

Thousands of dollars were spent by the American government during the Vietnam era to evaluate wartime use of helicopters for a variety of purposes. The conclusion was that helicopters are a viable part of military operations, but should not be used indiscriminately.

Of all aircraft, helicopters are considered the most machinelike. They rely on lots of big, moving parts, and are said to beat the air into submission rather than fly through it. In simple terms, a helicopter flies because its rotor blades accelerate a column of air downward that weighs more than the aircraft. This produces a reaction that pushes the helicopter up.

Pilots contend there is nothing effortless about handling a helicopter. It can react at times like a child with a mind of its own, and that, of course, is where the challenge lies in flying one.

It's also where the fear comes in for nurses, paramedics, and even patients who are at the mercy of the aircraft and its pilot. . . .

For the most part, the aircraft is a way for us to get somewhere quickly. But there are times when you're scared shitless. There are so many more variables to worry about than when you're riding in the back of an ambulance.

I don't think about quitting this job, but I think about crashing. I don't like to fly with new pilots, or when it's bad weather. I think a lot of people are like me, more afraid of flying than they will admit.

Sometimes you're flying along and you don't know if something is going wrong. What scares me is when the pilot starts cussing. You'll hear, "Shit!" or "Goddammit!" and you don't know whether he's annoyed at something or a part just fell off the plane.

In this case, the pilot scared himself as well as his crew:

We were taking off from the top of a building at one of the nearby hospitals when we encountered a wind tunnel. Suddenly the winds rose to about fifty-five mph, and as we lifted off, the helicopter tilted and turned sideways.

We had a new doctor on board, and I grabbed

his hand. We swooped down as the pilot strug-
gled to regain control. He did, and we soon
leveled out, but he was so scared, he couldn't
land. We flew around for a while so he could
compose himself. Then we were called to a
scene.

The pilot said, "I can't go. I have to land."

The doctor—who had tears in his eyes—swore
he'd never fly again.

The pilot told me later it was the closest he
had ever come to crashing. If we had been in a
smaller helicopter, he said, the wind would have
forced us into the building.

When patients express their fear of flying, there is
little nurses and paramedics can do except offer comfort and support:

You can tell when a patient is scared to fly.
He'll say, "I don't know if I want to do this or
not." Then he'll grab the stretcher tight. At times
like that, touch is very important. I'll hold hands
with the person, whether an adult or a child. All
they want is a little extra reassurance they aren't
going to die.

We've all had patients nervous about flying.
So you end up focusing on that and trying to
alleviate their anxiety. Sometimes people are not
used to the shimmying that is a normal part of
the helicopter ride. Other patients think flying is
the greatest thing in the world—when they're not
sick.

* * *

# FLIGHT FOR LIFE

I remember answering the call at the office to take a transfer patient from one outlying hospital to another. He was critically ill, but wide-awake and alert. As we were walking out the door, the phone rang again, and I almost didn't go back to answer it. When I did, it was the hospital telling us our call was canceled.

I thought the patient must have suddenly died.

But that wasn't the case.

"He won't go in your helicopter," we were told. "He says he won't have anything to do with it. He's going to be transported by ambulance."

"Did you explain the risk to him?" I asked.

"Yes, but he says he has made up his mind. He'll take his chances on the ground."

So I said, "Oh, well. You know? I guess there's nothing we can do."

You can lead a horse to water . . .

Developing a healthy respect for flying, without letting it interfere with their jobs, is one of the ways nurses and paramedics cope with the daily risks of being airborne:

I'd much rather fly in a helicopter than ride in the back of an ambulance. That's like being bounced around in a cardboard box. It makes me want to throw up.

I don't have a real fear of flying. But I have a real respect for it. You have to realize this job could kill you. But so can driving down the freeway.

\*     \*     \*

139

Whenever any one of us in the business goes down, it hurts. Every day, before I come to work, there's this little voice that reminds me: "Kiss your wife. Kiss your child. Tell them you love them before you leave."

That voice says what I'm doing here is dangerous, and I just want to make sure I leave on good terms.

I think about something happening, though I've never had a call where I thought, "Oh no, this is it."

Our pilots show excellent judgment, and I trust them with my life—literally.

We were called to an Indian reservation in California on a dark night, in a valley with no lights.

I thought, "We can't land here. We can't see a thing."

The pilot agreed and we didn't go in. That was our decision, one that may have saved our lives.

This nurse rationalizes the risk factors involved in flying in order to come to terms with its inherent dangers:

I travel sixty-four miles round trip on the interstate to get to work daily, and I think my chances of dying are much greater there. At least in a helicopter, I'll be doing something I like and the end will be quick and painless, rather than being, say, pinned inside a car.

FLIGHT FOR LIFE

A paramedic uses this approach:

I deal with the fear by thinking it won't happen to me. When I'm up there, I'm invincible. That's how I come back to work the next day.

And a flight nurse, grown weary by the sheer act of fighting her anxiety, simply turned it off:

I had never been in a helicopter before when I took this job. Ironically, I was afraid of flying, having gone through a bad-weather experience in a commercial airliner.

So I had a hard time getting used to going up in the air on a routine basis. If anyone had told me I would be flying for a living, I would have said, "No way."

I spent five years being afraid. Then one day I said, "This is bullshit. I *have* to get around in the air. So I'd better get over it." I talked myself out of my constant state of apprehension. And gradually I got past it. Now I love the flying.

Even after an accident in which the entire crew was hurt, a flight nurse injured in a crash either hid, or somehow overcame, her fear of flying:

I was late for work that morning and was hurrying into the parking lot when I saw our helicopter, flopped over on its side on the pad. My heart jumped. One of my friends was on duty, and I thought she might have been on board.

I ran upstairs and asked first thing, "Was any-

141

one killed?'' They said no, but there were injuries. The pilot, paramedic, and my friend, a flight nurse, were all in intensive care. Each one had a broken back.

She returned to work eleven months later. I never heard her say she was afraid, or wouldn't fly again.

Flight crews admit the issue of safety on the job is brought home with a vengeance after an accident or close call:

Everyone skirts around the issue of flying, and no one wants to talk about its inherent dangers. Then the phone rings and someone from another program says, "We just had a forced landing," or "We just put one into the side of a mountain and everyone is gone."

That's when it hits us that if that helicopter goes down, we're probably going to be dead.

You can't go out there thinking you're going to die. But it's there, in the back of your mind. There's a "Who's next?" mentality when anyone in a program has a problem. My first thought after a crash is, "Is our number up? Are we playing the odds?"

Most of us have lost friends through flying. But professionally, if you think you're going to crash, you won't make it in this business.

What you do instead is talk about it, go over every detail of a crash and find out how you can learn from other people's mistakes.

A few nurses and paramedics swear they do not suffer from fear of flying, and scoff at those who do:

Working a wreck on the interstate is a lot more dangerous to me than flying in a helicopter. I worry a lot more about getting hit by a tractor trailer while I'm bent over a patient on the side of the road.

I once worked with a nurse who was hyper about flying. The panel inside the helicopter had all these lights, and one kept coming on that wasn't supposed to.

About halfway to our destination, the pilot starts turning the helicopter around. And my nurse starts freaking out.

I thought, "What is going *on* here? What's wrong with these people?"

Our pilot wasn't the calmest person in the world, and he wouldn't talk to us. So I got on the radio and told the hospital we were coming back.

The behavior I saw was just incredible. A pilot who's nervous and a nurse who panics.

I spent the remainder of the flight devoting my time to taking care of them. Thank God the *patient* was stable.

I don't like ambulances, the way they speed around curves and down busy streets. I'll take a nice, safe helicopter anytime.

Yet close calls happen in the air, and when they do, they can make even the most seasoned flyer sit up and take notice:

> We were transporting a cardiac patient from a small town in North Carolina back to our hospital. About five minutes from our landing time, the tower tells us there are no aircraft between us and the hospital. Thirty seconds later we spot this Cessna 172, and it comes zooming past our window. The pilot was so close, I could actually see the cut of his brown hair and the red tie he was wearing.
>
> Now, *that's* a bit too close for comfort. We all got scared.

Flight teams say they seldom expose their families to details about the job that would cause them undue worry. But when the spouse or family member is in the medical profession, too, there is little they don't already know:

> My wife always makes a point of saying to me, "Be careful" whenever I leave the house. She worked here part time as a flight nurse when the program started, and she's aware of the risks involved. I wasn't in the profession at the time, and so I worried about her safety.
>
> Then I came to work here, and she phased out. She offered to return part time again, and I said, "No. One of us flying around in a helicopter is enough."
>
> That's not really fair, because I know she'd like to come back to work. Yet, that's how I

feel. It's okay for me to take chances, but not both of us.

The effects of flying for a living, and the problems and dangers it entails, often follow the flight team member far beyond the initial scene or patient transport. That's what happened to this chief flight nurse, who still wonders if the chances he takes are worthwhile:

It was nighttime and we were flying to a small hospital to pick up a patient with a "triple A" [abdominal aortic aneurysm] on the verge of rupturing. That's a weak spot in a major artery that bulges outward, like a hose with too much water pressure, ready to burst. We needed to get him to a cardiovascular surgeon like *right now* or the patient would die.

The weather was pretty bad as we headed out. Because of cloud cover, we couldn't make a direct approach, and I remember Paul, our pilot, saying, "Well, we can skirt around and come in on the back side—maybe."

I kept thinking, "Man, I hope we're not flying right into the middle of that lousy weather."

But we were getting closer and closer to it. We flew over a cliff, and I suddenly felt the earth fall away. Paul, however, leaned back and said nonchalantly, "We just spit right over that one, didn't we?"

As we passed through a cloud, we could see the lighted field below, our predesignated landing site about three miles from the local hospital. Coming in, Paul informed us we had exactly five minutes to get in and out, or we'd be grounded for the night because of weather.

As soon as we reached the ground, we ran to the ambulance that was waiting for us—literally sprinted to it—jumped in the back, and took off, lights spinning and sirens blaring.

My partner and I were nervous about the weather, so we kept looking out the window to check on conditions. We got to the hospital, jumped out, ran in and grabbed our patient, checked his pressure, and pushed him back out the door on a stretcher. We got him in the ambulance and back to the helicopter in a total of seven minutes flat. The helicopter was still running.

My basic concern now was transporting the patient—and us—back alive. Weather conditions were marginal at best, and getting worse.

At one point during the return flight, all the lights went out in the aircraft. Visibility was so bad outside, the pilot needed a darkened situation so he could attempt to see the ridge lines of the mountains up ahead, so he turned our cabin lights off. Imagine driving at night in your car with no lights inside or out, knowing you're headed towards an obstacle, but not knowing where it is.

Since I couldn't see to use our monitoring equipment, I had to keep my hand on the patient's neck to check his carotid pulse.

It was pitch-black and deathly quiet in the cabin. I looked outside and could still see absolutely nothing. Suddenly Paul said to us from the pilot's seat, "We're out of skill. We're running on luck now."

"There's a ridge line out there somewhere," I

told my partner. "I just hope we're high enough to miss it."

We knew there was a power line somewhere, too, but we were too far into the flight to turn around and go back.

Our patient was hanging in there, but there was little I could do medically under those conditions. If I didn't help serve as a lookout for the pilot, and we all went down, it wouldn't make any difference what I had done for the patient. We'd still all be dead.

The flight was twenty minutes, but seemed like two days. When we finally landed safely, I was totally stressed out.

I had a volleyball match that night, and as coach, I was especially hard on the players. At one point someone pulled me aside and said, "What is your problem?"

I couldn't explain it, but I was mad, confused, full of self-doubts about whether the decisions we had made were right. Under those conditions, should we have even made the flight? I was also scared, because I knew how close we had come, what chances we had taken.

I couldn't even talk to my girlfriend because I didn't know how to express all these mixed-up emotions. I just knew it was driving me nuts.

It took me days to get over it, asking myself over and over, "Was it worth it?" And I still don't know.

The decision making that goes into a flight procedure depends on one person. And flight crews know if he makes a wrong decision, a poor judgment call, a bad move, they could all go down.

That's why nurses and paramedics love him, hate him, fear him, and respect him all at the same time— little of which has much to do with him as an individual.

It is the complex role he plays that sets him apart from the other members of the helicopter medical team. For on every call, on every flight, he holds their lives within his hands.

He is different from the rest. He is the pilot.

# 8

# *Pilots*

*"We're at a scene and we've just saved the patient's life. We're exhausted, covered in blood, tubing and IV lines everywhere. Then someone runs up to us and says, 'Excuse me, are you the pilot?' 'No, he's over there, waiting for us.' 'Great! I want to get his autograph.' "*

—Chief flight nurse

BY THEIR OWN ADMISSION, PILOTS ARE A BREED apart. If they were doctors, they'd be surgeons, who—like pilots—are take-charge, go-get-'em types, rushing in to save a patient. Most have healthy egos and wear their air of confidence as comfortably as they wear their helmets. That's a generalization, of course, but pilots and the people they fly with agree it's an accurate overall assessment.

Nearly all flight nurses and paramedics have favorite stories they are eager to share that illustrates why pilots are labeled with tags such as "arrogant" or "egomaniac." It is part of the good-natured ribbing found in the team's daily interaction.

"I remember our pilot was always the first one through the door when we got to the hospital," recalled a chief flight nurse. "One time I walked in and the doctor was talking to him. He's listening

149

intently, hand on his hip, gazing over his glasses at the doctor.

"By the time I arrive, the physician has basically finished his patient report—to the *pilot!*

"So the pilot turns to the doctor and says, 'Well, Doc, you might want to tell *him* what you just told *me.*'"

Yet in all fairness, the perception of pilots as loose canons, on the ground or in the air, is nothing more than that—a perception, seldom rooted in reality. By necessity, pilots of all types must be well trained and disciplined to get, and keep, a job that requires them to control intricate machines under what are often high-stress conditions. According to helicopter pilots—some of whom contend they are the "second-class citizens in aviation,"—they are less understood, but subject to more stress, than fixed-wing pilots.

"We have skills that the average fixed-wing pilot can't touch," says a Virginia pilot who flew helicopters in Vietnam, "under conditions that most of these guys wouldn't consider flying in."

As a result, helicopter pilots have often been called the "cowboys" of aviation. The truth is, they counter, nothing in their work is left to chance.

"It's not like we're mavericks out there doing crazy rolls past the tower," says one experienced helicopter pilot. "That's not the way it is. In fact, any pilot who pulled a stunt like that would lose his wings after the first pass. Yeah, there might be a little cowboy in some of us, but it's deeply hidden and strictly controlled. As a group, we are professionals."

They also maintain they are underpaid and underrated compared to general aviation pilots, despite the fact that they work in high-risk environments, maneuvering a machine that's less stable and requires more technical skills than a fixed-wing aircraft.

While a corporate fixed-wing pilot can easily top $45,000 a year in exchange for less than a forty-hour week, medevac helicopter pilots seldom get above the $30,000 range. And unlike flight nurses, who can always transfer to another part of the hospital, the helicopter pilot often works on a short-term contract. If a flight program is not in demand, then neither is he. As a result, most say they are in it for the challenge of flying, rather than the security or the size of a paycheck.

One pilot says he loves flying a helicopter because "it's the closest you can come to being a bird." In fact, *the bird* is a frequent synonym pilots use for the aircraft.

Flying a helicopter is different from cruising along in commercial airliners, mostly because helicopters are less stable than other types of aircraft, and therefore more difficult to fly. It is also why safety is an issue that comes up time and again regarding helicopter flights.

Aviation writer Peter Garrison says there are pilots who think too much appreciation of risks makes a bad pilot, and that safety in flying is "an elastic idea."

"Flying requires either a blind (and dumb) belief in the reliability of man-made equipment," he states, "or a kind of unconscious abandon, like that of charging troops."

Where is the line, he asks, between reckless actions in the air and the honorable, necessary pursuit of one's duty in a hazardous occupation?

Flight nurses and paramedics, who cannot answer that question, must instead forge an unspoken bond of trust between themselves and the pilot. In a sense, it is an interdependent relationship. In the air, crew members are the pilot's extra eyes and ears. On the ground, he is their extra pair of hands.

It is this mutual trust that holds the pilot and crew together, forming the basis for a viable working relationship. When that bond is broken, the relationship falls apart. A paramedic describes one such experience. . . .

We took off one morning about four-thirty to pick up a patient diagnosed with an abdominal aneurysm that was leaking. We got about ten miles from takeoff and saw a mountain. I knew the town where we were going had hills, but no mountains.

So I said to the pilot, "Is that a mountain up ahead?"

"Yeah," he answered.

I noticed we were climbing, then descending, and I realized we were lost. I finally told him, "Hey, it's okay if we're lost, but tell me so I can call and arrange for an ambulance for the patient wherever we land." The dispatcher heard me on the radio, so to save face, I told him we had hit some heavy rain and we were detouring.

We started coming down—to the left and then to the right. The flight nurse and I knew which direction to go, but our pilot wasn't listening to us. He kept turning left, then right.

Dispatch was tracking us and wanted to know

what the hell was going on. By then we had officially aborted the flight and called ahead for ambulance transport for the patient. We couldn't
yet tell Dispatch where we were going to land
because we didn't know, but we told them to
stand by.

We were real low, and the airport tower ra-
dioed to us, "Are you going to climb to so-and-
so feet?"

The pilot wouldn't answer. We were flying at
twelve hundred feet, and the towers were fifteen
hundred feet high.

The controller then came back over the radio
and said, "I *suggest* you climb!"

We climbed to twenty-five hundred feet, and
somehow found our way back to the heliport. All
the way back, the flight nurse and I held hands.
I told her I was going to kiss the ground when
we got there. Instead, when we landed, I wanted
to hit the pilot. And I probably could have gotten
away with it, because everyone else wanted to
hit him, too. Next time out, we refused to fly
with him. So did several other people, which dis-
rupted our entire team.

Pilots who hear that story say it only takes one
experience with a "bad pilot" to discredit "good pilots" who handle themselves, their colleagues, and
the aircraft with the utmost care and respect.

"These people are my work family," says a Florida
pilot, "so I'm not going to put them at risk with fool-
ish, reckless behavior. Still, we recognize it takes
time and effort to earn that kind of trust."

One pilot, new to a hospital program in North Carolina, learned that lesson early on. The chief flight

nurse who accompanied the pilot to pick up a patient in an adjoining county recounts the story:

At first, when you're with a new pilot, you're always wondering, "What's this guy gonna do next?" So you watch him pretty closely the first few times you go out.

We were headed to a neighboring hospital to pick up our patient when something went wrong with my headset. I couldn't hear what was transpiring over the radio, but I looked out the window and suddenly I realized we were turning away from our destination. I didn't want to jump the pilot on the spot as if to say, "Hey, do you not know where you're going?" but as we began approaching our home hospital, I thought, "God, he thinks *this* is the neighboring hospital! He's completely turned around."

I knew where we were supposed to be, so I finally said, "I'm not trying to tell you what to do, but I don't think we made the right turn."

"Yeah, I know that," he answered.

I wasn't sure what to say at that point.

He let me sit in silence for a few more minutes, wondering what the hell was going on, then he told me the flight had been aborted—the patient didn't need transport after all. I could have killed him. Then I got to know him better and trust his judgment. So when something similar happens now, I sit back and enjoy the ride. I know he knows what he's doing.

Regardless of how strong the bond, or how good the working relationship between pilots and their crew, clashing of egos and differences of opinion eventually erupt, especially when it comes to flight versus medical decisions. Few pilots tolerate back-seat drivers, for example.

"If a crew member questions my decision to fly, that really rubs me the wrong way," says one seasoned pilot. "My attitude is, don't tell me how to fly and I won't tell you how to do medicine."

"There are a couple of crew members who always look at you when anything minor happens, like they're panicked," says a California pilot. "They are just not comfortable flying. So you take them aside and say, 'Look, what are you going to do when there's a *real* problem? If you don't like to fly, what the hell are you doing here?' "

Helicopter pilots pride themselves on their skill and good judgment, and won't let *anyone* tell them how to do their job. A New York pilot describes one such experience. . . .

People believe you need a forty-acre field to put this ship on the ground. You'd think it was a damn 747. But you don't require a lot of space, especially in daylight when you can see all the obstacles ahead.

I landed in a street one night, where a police officer had been shot. The landing zone was extremely small. There was another helicopter flying above it, so I got on the radio to talk to the other pilot.

"You're wasting your time," he told me. "You'll never get in there."

That was the wrong thing to say.

When I landed the aircraft, the nurse opened

the door, got out, took two steps, and kneeled down to the patient. It was *that* close.

It is the pilot who sets the tone for the entire crew, say flight members. If panic sets in, for whatever reason, it is infectious, and it is often up to the pilot to control it. The same holds true with personality conflicts.

"I've had nurses and paramedics screaming at each other over what kind of treatment to give to a patient," says a New Jersey pilot. "I even had one nurse yell at me for asking a question. I didn't interrupt at the time, because it might have harmed the patient, but later I told her, 'Don't ever do that again or I won't fly with you anymore. I won't tolerate that on my aircraft.' "

"There's a lot of territorialism in piloting and a certain amount of power play," a flight paramedic agreed. "But it works both ways. If the pilot gets in our face, interfering with our job, we tell him to shut the hell up, and if we interfere in his, he tells us the same."

Others use humor to get their point across.

"We're always bugging our pilot about the weather," says a North Carolina flight nurse. "We want to know what it's doing that day, whether we're flying or not, what's gonna happen. So now he comes in and just makes a daily announcement: 'There will be light followed by occasional darkness.' "

Nurses and paramedics get their payback. Pranks and good-natured ribbing are a daily part of the conversational flow in the average flight team program. Comeuppance is quick, relentless, evidenced by standard jokes: "What separates a flight nurse from the lowest form of life known?"

Answer: "The back of the pilot's seat."

But coupled with the camaraderie in a flight team is an earnest awareness of when to turn serious, when to get back down to business. It is when the beeper goes off, indicating a flight is imminent, or when the flight team is airborne, ready to head for a scene, that lighthearted banter is either cast aside or used to minimize the impact of whatever trauma awaits.

Once ensconced in the aircraft, each pilot has his own method of flying. His crew members know that when there's any deviation in style, it's usually a warning there's trouble at hand.

One flight nurse looks for broken silences when flying with a normally reticent pilot.

"When he says, 'Don't worry' about five times in a row, then I worry," she says.

Among the recipes for disaster are mechanical failures and obstacle strikes. Bird strikes, for example—flocks of screeching, panicked fowls smashing into the windshield of the aircraft—occur primarily during clear weather. Most take place in May and October, when birds tend to migrate. The windshield or canopy where the pilot is sitting is the most common site of impact, but a bird strike anywhere on or near the aircraft can create a dangerous distraction.

Weather is the most common cause for concern, accounting for the majority of aborted flights, and can be a pilot's worst enemy, challenging even the most skilled and professional airman.

Ric, mid-thirties, is the quintessential pilot. All-American handsome, with a square-jawed face and wide grin, set on a body sculpted by regular work-outs, he has the look and demeanor of the classic aviator. When he is in dark glasses and bomber jacket, one can almost see him posed, silhouetted against the sky, ready for takeoff. When not flying, he is bored, restless, pacing the floor with suppressed energy. Like most pilots, he is assertive, opinionated, and slightly left of center. His symbol of unconventionality is a gold stud he wears in one ear.

His high school yearbook records a long-term fascination with flying, one that followed him into the army. A stint manning helicopters in the Gulf of Mexico gave him stateside experience, though most of his flying took place in North Carolina.

Originally from New Jersey, he has settled into the Blue Ridge Mountains in North Carolina for now. As lead pilot with a hospital-based flight team program, he has a reputation among the flight crew for steady nerves and reliability. He is, in other words, a solidly good pilot.

Yet even he gets foiled by nature's forces from time to time. To his credit, he is the first to admit it. In remembering his closest call flying in the mountains, he moves forward in his chair, his body tenses, and his eyes grow brighter.

"We got a request to go to an accident scene for an elderly lady who had been hit by a car. Between our takeoff point and our destination, we had to fly over Mount Mitchell, the highest peak east of the Rockies. I was aware of the warnings to stay away from the area because of turbulence. With the sharp rise of the peak, all the wind currents go up, then revert, brought back down by other currents. Therefore, you get this rolling effect. I did not make a conscious decision to ignore the warnings. In fact, I never really thought we were at risk. And I wanted to go the quickest route possible. So I chose to fly straight through.''

Ric, the flight nurse, and a paramedic reached a thousand feet above Mount Mitchell when suddenly the helicopter began to rise and fall.

"It was like a damn roller coaster ride," says Ric.

"We shouldn't be here," he thought, passing the mountain's summit.

Everyone fell silent so he could concentrate.

Marty, the paramedic, knew Ric's body language and could tell there was a problem.

"He's usually pretty relaxed," says Marty, "but he was leaning forward, almost on top of the panel, and real tense. It was like he was trying to see everything in front of him at once."

Atop the aircraft, now tossing and turning, the rotor blades whined ominously, straining against the pressure of uneven currents. Too much pressure on the rotors and they could separate from the ship— literally break off—making the helicopter drop like a rock.

The sound made Marty go white.

Instinctively Ric searched for the ground. But he knew he couldn't land without crashing, for there was nowhere to go but into the steep, forbidding side of the mountain. The only way out was straight up.

"Okay, idiot," he admonished himself. "You got yourself into this. Now get yourself out."

"I knew if I panicked, that would be the worst thing of all. So I mentally slapped myself and looked at what to do and how to do it, step by step."

Ric maneuvered the helicopter into position for a vertical rise, gunning the engine until the aircraft reached eighty-five hundred feet. By then, they were up and out of the currents. It took a full five minutes, but they were minutes that seemed like hours to Ric and the crew.

Later, after returning to home base, he was astonished to learn the winds had clocked 114 miles per hour that day at Mount Mitchell.

"I hadn't flown in the mountains before," he said, "and I didn't understand all of the dynamics of what I was doing going in. I now know there are places that will clean your clock if you're not careful. And I know, too, that I'll never trust the mountains and their unpredictable conditions again."

Ric encountered engine failure on another routine flight, but this time it was the crew that panicked, not him.

"We went to a small community hospital to get a patient who was going downhill rapidly. When we arrived, the nurse and paramedic ran inside to get him. I turned off the aircraft, and when they came back outside, I could tell they wanted to move fast. So I started the first engine. No problem. But the second engine wouldn't fire.

"I glanced back at my crew, with this very sick patient on board, and they had looks of despair in their eyes. They watched me while I got out, opened the cowling, and tapped on the starter. Both thought I had gone crazy because they didn't think you could tinker with a helicopter and make it start. Then the engine fired, and I got back in my seat.

"You guys ready to go?" I asked.

"They just sat there, looking dumbfounded. We got the patient back to our home base, though, and he fully recovered."

Every pilot agrees there are times he will make errors in judgment. Some will even go out on a limb and say the majority of accidents that occur are due to pilot error. With experience, even the most technically skilled pilot learns to say no, he won't go, when a proposed flight doesn't meet his guidelines for safety. There are conditions, however, and problems that are beyond his ability to predict, or his capability to control. These are the variables he must deal with, on and off the ground:

In Texas we keep a close eye on the weather and the power lines. Those are our biggest obstacles. One minute you can have beautiful weather, and fifteen miles ahead, you can't see your hand in front of your face.

Our hospitals don't always understand that. You'll be talking to them by radio and the communicator will say, "Well, *I'm* outside and I can see the *stars.*"

And you'll say, "Well, *I'm* outside—sixty feet up—and I can't see the *ground.*"

If weather at our destination is lousy, we don't go in. If you push it, you're going to get yourself in trouble.

\*     \*     \*

We have two months a year where we really have to be concerned with fog, and those two months wear on us.

Overall, we have easy flying conditions—other than migratory birds. There's not a safe altitude in this part of Texas where you don't have to worry about birds.

I hit a hawk once and it got sucked into the air intake [that part of the helicopter where the air goes into the engine]. It completely destroyed a piece of sheet metal. If that bird had been three feet lower, it would have come through the windshield. We're talking five pounds of dead weight at 150 miles per hour.

Sometimes we have thousands of egrets that fly in flocks. They play follow the leader and present special hazards, especially at night. If they lose sight of their leader, they frenzy, and go into a panic.

When that happens, they don't look for you, or at you. We call it a bird strike. And they are deadly.

In other parts of the land, it's a different kind of animal that's deadly to pilots:

There are New York City pilots and then there's everyone else. You've got to know what you're doing or you don't belong here. There's a tremendous amount of helicopter traffic around the city, so much that it takes a new pilot at least a month or two just to get used to traffic control. We have five major airports in a relatively small area, each with different routes and checkpoints.

Many times you have to talk, think, and listen on two different frequencies.

Then there are the streets below to contend with. It's not unusual in some parts of New York City for us to hear gunfire near the spot where we're coming in to land.

It makes me a little nervous to get around scenes where there are a lot of bystanders. Our helicopter weighs sixty-seven hundred pounds, and that's a heavy object blowing a lot of debris.

You think a leaf blower cleans up—you should see what we do to parking lots!

When a serious problem arises, pilots say they like to think they react like airmen in the movies—suave, debonair, unruffled. What's closer to the truth is that they may be quaking inside, but their training and methodical approach take over:

I had a fuel control failure and the engine started running away on me.

I knew from experience that the crew members I had on board were the type who would ask questions when things started going wrong. So as soon as I realized I had a problem, I told them all to sit down and be quiet, that I was going to declare an emergency. There would be no more questions and no running around in the back of the aircraft. I had a lot of analyzing to do.

We had a patient on board, and typically my response in a situation like that is to get the patient to his destination as quickly as possible. But in this case, I could barely control the engine and didn't know how to correct the problem. So I had no choice but to turn around and go to the nearest airport.

I had about five miles to fly and a lot of figuring out to do. I also had a lot of calls to make: to the hospital, letting them know we had an emergency; to the tower, so they could divert traffic. Each of them had their own set of questions. My priority was the tower, because they were the controlling agent.

Which runway did I want?

Should they roll out the emergency equipment?

At the same time, I'm trying to figure out why I've got this equipment in the off position and it's still running. And if the bad engine is running, why is the good one lying down? Is *this* engine the good one, or the bad one?

Now the tower is bugging me again, wanting to know which runway I wanted. But I didn't want to be bothered with that kind of question at the moment. I wanted to be left alone so I could figure out what the hell was going on.

I finally got us down safely, but my major concern was why? What went wrong and why did this happen? I started out as an aircraft mechanic, and every time something happens on board, I always have to know why.

We try to learn from what takes place after a crash or a close call, but we can't go worrying about it all the time or we won't be effective. We understand it's inherent in the business that some things will go wrong. So we just do our job as safely as we can.

In this scene call, it was the weather that went wrong, underscoring the unpredictability that is part of every pilot's working day and the decisions he is forced to make:

We were en route to Myrtle Beach to pick up a cardiac patient who was stable but needed a quick flight rather than a long ambulance ride.

It was summer, and thunderstorms were common in the area that time of year. We got a good forecast before we left, refueled in Florence, South Carolina, and I called the weather service again because I noticed a buildup of cumulus clouds.

I got another good forecast and we took off for the relatively short flight to Myrtle. As I'm climbing out of Florence, I'm talking to approach control and I say, "Looks like there's some thunderstorms out there on radar."

The tower responds, "Oh, didn't you know about convective sigmet echo?" That's a warning issued to aircrafts indicating dangerous meteorological conditions such as thunderstorms or severe air turbulence.

I said no.

Now we're 180 miles into this 200-mile flight and I discover there's a line of thunderstorms right in front of us. Do I abort the flight? I can see the coastline ahead, so no, I'm not going to abort the flight.

We're flying along and bullshitting and all of a sudden, out of a dark cloud close to us, comes this big bolt of lightning—and I'm about to fly right through it. So I go around and another bolt comes out of the other cloud beside it.

There's not a drop of rain and you can't hear any thunder, just these bolts out of the blue. I fly right between them.

We got into Myrtle Beach and landed and here comes this line of thunderstorms. It was 1:00 P.M. and they didn't dissipate until 7:00 P.M.

There are few things I won't do, but one of them is to fly through a line of thunderstorms at night. What could happen is a "mircroburst," a tremendous downdraft that starts sucking air around it. If you don't have enough power to get out of it, you're history. And you can't always see it till you're in it.

Needless to say, we stayed at Myrtle Beach that night.

That was one flight that got my attention.

Pilots learn to respect nature, for their own safety and the safety of their passengers.

I'll admit I've pushed the weather further than I should have. But now I won't fly unless I can see the ground. I've turned around midflight, gone back and called a ground ambulance, and had them transport the patient. Then I slept in the back of the helicopter till it got light.

It's frustrating when you get put on hold because of the weather, especially when you know there's an 85 to 90 percent chance you can make it if you leave right away. It's a gray area, and one that causes us a lot of headaches in exercising judgment. If we make the flight with no problem, no one says anything about it.

But if we go, and something screws up so that

we can't finish the flight, administration comes back and says, "Why did you go in the first place?"

That's when I say, "I'm just doing my job."


Part of doing their job, say pilots, is keeping their mind and attention on flying, rather than on the patient they must transport. Most prefer not to get involved in patient care at all, other than playing the role of driver. For some it is a form of self-defense, a shield that protects them from overinvolvement in somebody else's despair.

That shield is normally not cracked until a child is injured or ill, or a patient comes along who somehow, some way, strikes a chord:


I remember one young girl, a high school student, who landed under a vehicle in a wreck. Her mother's maiden name was the same as mine, and she was from the same part of the country I was from.

The girl was paralyzed from the neck down, and I took a special interest in her, keeping up with her recovery.

One day she called me to her room and said she had something to show me. Her index finger on her left hand was moving. That's how her recovery started.

She graduated from high school lying in a hospital bed, went on to recover, and eventually got a degree in broadcast journalism.

In a sense, I felt like her father, watching her change from a helpless child to an adult. It was very gratifying, and a very unusual experience for me.

We went into the flight fat, dumb, and happy, not knowing what it was about. The case was a transfer of a little girl about my daughter's age, who had been diagnosed with spinal meningitis.

I was standing around waiting to help load the child, and turned to ask the therapist where she would be in the hospital so I could visit her tomorrow.

"That's not possible," she said.

"Why not?"

"Because the family is making her funeral arrangements right now. She won't make it past today."

It hit me like a ton of bricks. I realized then I couldn't let myself get involved every time I flew a patient, because it hurts too much. There are too many people we bring back who die.

It took a long time for me to get over that "baby flight." I knew I had to learn to deal with it or get out of it altogether.

My wife didn't want to hear about death on the job, so I had no support system there. I went out and got drunk instead.

The first time I flew a child as a patient really hurt. When you know they've been a missile shot out of a Jeep at sixty mph, there's no black humor there. There's only pain.

Each flight is different, so it has its own value that you store away, something unique you get out of it. But there is one big misconception.

People think we're the answer to their survival—
their only answer.

I've sat in the helicopter many times and heard
people say, "Well, Uncle Joe's gonna be okay
because the team is here." Uncle Joe may be
99.9 percent dead, and there's nothing we can do
to bring him back. But they're all at ease because
we're there.

As for me, I don't save lives. I fly helicopters.

Whatever the conflicts, whatever the problems and
misconceptions pilots must bear, they are an integral
part of the flight crew team, and like nurses and paramedics, want nothing more than to be understood:

As pilots, I don't think we always get the recognition we deserve. We're professionals, but a lot
of people see us as these young, mad technicians.

It's especially true when an aircraft crashes
and the press comes in. All they want to report
are the bad things. You never hear about us making
the paper when we had a very pleasant flight and
nothing went wrong, or we took some kid to the
hospital and everything turned out fine.

In fact, our local paper never mentions our
name unless we do something wrong.

We hear the complaints that we don't work
hard enough, that we sit around or take naps
when we're not flying. But I'm not getting paid
to work all the time. I'm getting paid for when
they call me.

It's like the joke about the computer that
breaks down and the guy comes in and takes a

hammer and hits it. Then he charges four hundred dollars.

"That's bullshit," he's told. "Why four hundred dollars?"

"Let me itemize," he explains. "It's five dollars to hit it, and three hundred ninety-five for knowing *where* to hit it."

That's what we do. We know how to fly the aircraft and when to fly it. And it's that expertise for which we're paid.

# 9
# *Flights from Hell*

*"You fall on the stairs getting into the helicopter, reach for a chart that's not there, run out of IV fluid, or find out you have to hike a mile to a scene call. That's when you know it's going to be a bad day."*

—Greg,
chief flight nurse

THERE ARE TIMES, SAY FLIGHT PERSONNEL, WHEN Murphy's Law is sitting on their shoulder, ready to dog their path like a midday shadow. The helicopter cranks, then sputters, the radio mysteriously stops working, the flight team—in a collective snit—can't get their act or their motor skills together. Supplies slip out of their hands, words not meant to be said come tumbling out, weather unexpectedly turns ugly. The patient is stable when they arrive, then suddenly worsens. Everything that can go wrong, does.

It's a rite of passage for rookie flight team members, an inevitable slice of the job for veterans.

"When you're brand-new," says a Houston paramedic, "you can't wait to go out on rescues. It's like the white knight syndrome. You think you're going to rush out and save all these lives every single time.

Then after a while, you find out that just doesn't happen. There are certain scene calls *no one* wants to be on, or calls they wish they had not taken. We label these our 'Flights from Hell.' It's a term everyone in the business knows well."

And sooner or later, he adds, it's something everyone in the business experiences.

Sometimes it's nothing more than a rough flight, which is bad enough, according to this Tennessee flight nurse:

The weather was lousy and the flight was long. We had two cardiac patients to pick up, which is difficult to deal with, because you've got double the number of intravenous lines and medications.

We arrived at the hospital, and the patients are in two different parts of the building, so it took us longer than we expected to load them. We finally got them settled in the helicopter and took off. The winds were strong, the weather cold and rough.

During the ride back, we were literally getting knocked around by the turbulence. I kept having to undo my seat belt to get up and adjust the IV lines for the patients and check their blood pressure, which was dropping on both. Not a good sign.

The patients said they were nauseated, so I reached over to get the airsick bag, and it's gone. I look back at my paramedic and he's white as a ghost, ready to throw up. He has the bag in his hand.

Now I'm starting to feel a little sick, too, but I can't find any more sick bags and I can't understand where they went. We always keep a supply on hand. I do locate one or two for the patients, but can't find any more.

I'm getting more nauseated by the minute, but I try to control it while I look after my patients. The paramedic is too ill to be of much help.

I couldn't wait to get on the ground, and I'm sure everyone else felt the same. After we landed, I decided I didn't want to fly again for quite a while. I don't think the patients did either.

Those are the kinds of flights you think will never end.

A Texas flight nurse recalls a particularly bad scene call involving a woman who was attacked in her home after she walked in on the man who had just stabbed her daughter to death. The assailant was an ex-convict the woman had hired to help her maintain an apartment complex she managed.

She was the ultimate flight patient because she was so critically hurt and needed transport fast. For me, it was a flight from hell because she had been stabbed dozens of times—always a horrible sight—and she didn't know her daughter was dead. So I had to deal with her fear and uncertainty, then her trauma when she found out. On top of all that, we were required to go to court and testify against the assailant. We hate it when we have to get involved in court cases. It's time-consuming, nerve-racking, and not something anybody on my flight team likes to do.

The good thing that can be said about "Flights from Hell" is that they don't happen very often, a fact demonstrated by the thousands of scene calls and transports that take place daily without mishap. Every scene call and patient transport is orchestrated with such a high degree of skill and expertise that even unexpected problems are dealt with before they deteriorate into anything resembling a disaster.

Despite the medical teams' best efforts, however, things do go wrong from time to time. And when that happens, it makes for a memorable flight. . . .

My partners and I got a call from the Blue Ridge Parkway that an elderly man had lost control of his van in the middle of a curve and had gone down a 210-foot embankment. His wife, who was seated on the passenger side, was reading a map at the time and he got distracted, losing control of the car.

The first paramedics on the scene detected a pulse on the man and were talking to him. They determined that the wife wasn't seriously hurt. They put a collar on the man and began to extricate him from the vehicle. At that moment he went into full cardiac arrest. That's when they called us.

Two news teams were there when we arrived, and they kept sticking cameras in our faces. It was an irritation, to say the least, and set the tone for this scene call.

We climbed down over the bank and found our patient, a huge man who weighed at least three hundred pounds. The ground crew was having trouble putting a tube down his throat so he could breathe. It was a miserably hot day and everyone was sweating like crazy as we tried to figure out how to get this enormous, very sick man up the mountain.

While my partner attempted to intubate him, I tried my first subclavian: inserting a control line that goes beneath the collarbone, allowing easier access for drug injection to the heart. But I blew it. I couldn't get the line in, and David couldn't get the tube in. So we were reduced to doing basic-level emergency medicine.

Next we began dragging him up the mountain, ten feet at a time, in ninety-degree temperatures and 100 percent humidity. We finally got him to the helicopter, but we had another problem. Ric, our pilot, weighs 190 pounds. David weighs the same. I weigh 210. And then we've got a three-hundred-pound-plus patient. We're overloaded.

Ric came across the intercom and said, "I don't know about this."

He's not the type of pilot to push the panic button, so I responded, "What are you talking about?"

"We're too heavy to lift off," he said. "But there is something I can try that might get us out of here."

"You're the driver," I said.

So we're up and going and then I heard this thud. I looked up and saw some kind of green shit flying all over the place. Because of our weight, we had hit a frigging pine tree. We were caught in a gap between two big trees, and Ric could only get about twenty feet off the ground.

We tried it again, and this time Ric literally

dove us off the ledge. Later someone who lived below said every window in his house shook as we flew over.

We got the patient to the hospital and he still didn't have an airway, a subclavian, or an IV. We felt totally incompetent. It was one of those times when everything we tried had gone awry.

The patient was dead as a wedge before we ever got him to the hospital, but we still had to do everything we possibly could.

The kicker was, we got to the hospital drenched in sweat, and three of our crew had to be treated for heat exhaustion. Then one of the emergency room nurses walked up to us, hands on her hips, and said, "If you guys are through flying around, come upstairs and help us do some *real* work."

One of medicine's pitfalls is that it is an inexact science, marked by variables and uncontrollable factors, one of which is that humans make mistakes. Unfortunately, when mistakes are made in medicine, the consequences can be deadly, as these novice flight nurses and interns found out:

I went with a new doctor to a scene call involving a fourteen-year-old boy who was horseback riding. He ran into a tree, was knocked to the ground, and injured his head. He looked okay, but he kept throwing up.

All my instincts told me to intubate this kid. But the doctor said, "No, I think he's fine. Let's get him on the helicopter."

We loaded him, and the pilot cranked the engine. Before we even got off the ground, the kid was throwing up again. Strapped down as he was, flat on his back, the fluid was sucking right back into his lungs. And that could kill him.

I thought, "Oh shit!" and yelled at the pilot, "Don't lift! We have an emergency situation."

We needed to turn the kid on his side, but the stretcher was strapped so tight, I couldn't get it loose. Meanwhile, this kid was beginning to die on us.

The pilot set us back down. "Turn off the aircraft!" I said.

Outside the helicopter, there were at least a hundred people at the scene, including the boy's mother. I knew I had to bring him out so we could intubate him and get him breathing again.

We unloaded him quickly and worked on him at the back of the aircraft. We couldn't get the tube down and he was going bad on us again. His heart rate and oxygen saturation dropped. I knew I had made the wrong decision when I did not intubate him at the beginning.

I tried to justify my actions—it was a short flight, he seemed okay, etc. But I knew that as flight nurse, the final responsibility was mine.

I let the doctor check to see why we couldn't get the tube in. I was about to cry, so afraid this child was going to die on us, his mother twenty feet away, yelling and screaming at us to save him.

Our last resort was to cut his throat, a procedure called a cricothyrotomy in which we slit the windpipe and insert a tube. Once you cut, you're committed. Your fingers go in to hold the opening and if you turn loose, you lose the hole in the skin and trachea and you have to start over again, which means critical time wasted.

I started the cut, and the doctor attempted to insert a tube. But it still wouldn't go in. I panicked, grabbed the doctor by the shirt, and said, "Get that fucking tube in! This kid's gonna die!"

He looked at me like I was crazy, and kept inserting the tube. It went up and up, and finally—thank god—slipped into the right place.

The kid's neck was cut from one end to the other, but once we got the tube in, he stabilized, his vital signs improved, and we got him loaded again, home free.

A week later, he had fully recovered.

But it took me much longer to get over the trauma. It was luck of the draw that we got the tube in. Otherwise, we would have lost him. And I would have quit over it, thinking, "This is it. I can't do anything right."

Even when you're new, you are still expected to know everything. One day we were flying to a scene in one of our smaller aircraft. I was new, the pilot was new, and the doctor with us was new. Our destination was a car wreck in an isolated area. It would have taken half an hour to get there by ambulance, so we were called instead.

First we got lost. I mean really lost. An ambulance could have made it to the scene and still had time to wait before we arrived.

Then our doctor got airsick. He was throwing up all over the helicopter. To top it off, the weather turned freezing cold.

We found the scene, landed, and upon checking the patient, discovered he had broken every bone in his face. He needed an airway, but I had never cut a person's throat and put a tube down.

The man, despite his injuries, was awake, and I was afraid to cut into his throat with no anesthesia, while he was still conscious. The doctor was no help. He was right out of med school and knew even less of emergency medicine than I did.

We couldn't fly the patient without an airway, because he would die. And that would be my fault.

So I decided to do the procedure with no help from anyone. I remember getting the knife out and starting to cut. I got through the skin and the patient began freaking out. He was awake and knew what was going on. I couldn't cut the trachea. I mean, can you imagine how painful that would be with no anesthesia? So I stopped and told the doctor let's load him as he is. My justification was that if he started to die, I could always finish the procedure while we were airborne.

We loaded him and lifted off, his throat partially cut. Then our pilot announced, "We're out of fuel. We're going to have to land somewhere else."

I thought, "Shit. What else can happen?"

My only hope was that we could get him to a nearby hospital, *they* could intubate him, and my hospital would never know what a mess I had made of this case.

But the pilot said, "We have to land at the airport."

"No!" I said. "He'll die if we don't get him to a hospital!" I was in a state of panic.

The pilot said he would see what he could do. We had ten minutes before we ran out of fuel.

The patient was momentarily stable, so I took the time to organize supplies in case he went bad on me again. I reached to get my medical bag containing all my emergency equipment, and realized it wasn't there.

I had left it at the scene!

If the patient started to die, I would be in the helicopter with virtually no equipment other than what we could find on hand. The patient would die and I would be fired. I was sure of it.

The pilot said he thought we could make it back to our hospital, but just barely.

I was almost in tears. It was a nightmare.

We got back to the hospital, and everyone agreed that no, I shouldn't have cut the skin. We got the patient into surgery, and he came out okay. I didn't do him any good, but I didn't do him any real harm either.

There were no repercussions, because no one knew the whole story. It's hard to tell anyone in our program about mistakes, because no one wants to admit to doing anything wrong. We're all supposed to be perfect. At least that's how I felt at the time.

Today I have more knowledge and confidence and would deal with the situation a lot differently, and with a lot more competence.

New flight team members aren't the only ones who botch a scene call or fail to do a necessary procedure.

Sometimes it happens even to the best and the most experienced nurse or paramedic:

You can get spooked and not be able to do a procedure even when you know you must. I had a victim of a car wreck whose face was nearly peeled off when we arrived. We put him in the aircraft, and when I went to intubate him, his entire facial structure moved.

I thought, "I can't do this. I just can't."

We "bagged" him instead [administered oxygen manually], and he started having irregular cardiac rhythms. So then we had to do full-blown CPR and administer medications.

It was one of those times when, in retrospect, I got angry at myself because I didn't try to go ahead and intubate. His whole face was rearranged and covered with so much blood and fluid, I could barely see what I was doing. Yet I still felt I should not have given up.

Nurses on every flight tend to do that—constantly second-guess themselves.

*Was there something else I could have done?* That question never gets fully answered.

In this scene call, the flight nurse was left to her own devices, while the support system around her failed:

We went to a small Texas town that had no ground crew paramedics, only basic-emergency-trained personnel.

We were called because it was an accident involving a mother and child needing certain procedures that their emergency crew are not allowed to do. When I walked up to the ambulance, there was a child on the stretcher with her skull split open. The other patient appeared more stable, so I directed my attention to the child. Nothing had been done.

I set up the face mask and IV and asked the doctor with me—a female intern just out of med school—to intubate while I got the IV started.

"I'm not comfortable with that," she said. "I've never intubated a child before."

I set up the face mask and said, "Then just keep bagging while I do the IV. At least we'll have an airway going."

Next I asked the doctor if she would tape the IV line securely while I worked on the child's airway. The pilot had stepped in at this point and was handing me things I needed, doing everything he could to help.

I looked down and the IV was running out on the floor. It had not been taped and had fallen out. I wasn't happy.

I couldn't trust anyone other than the pilot, who wasn't even medically trained, and I felt all alone with this very sick child on my hands.

I kept my anger bottled up because it's not professional to lash out at a scene. It takes time away from the patient. And if you alienate everyone around you, you'll get even less help than before.

What I wanted to say to the doctor was, "What *are* you comfortable doing?" Instead, I asked her to get back in the aircraft and sit there.

To make matters worse, the child ended up dying. I couldn't help wondering, if I'd had a good pair of hands to help me, would the outcome have been different?

It wasn't bad performance, but bad timing and circumstance that made this a "Flight from Hell":

It was Christmas day and our program was having trouble covering the shift, so my husband, who works with me, and I volunteered to help. Our call was to transfer a patient from one hospital to another.

When we got to the hospital, we realized this was not a viable patient. He weighed three hundred pounds and had a gunshot wound to the head—probable suicide.

He had IV lines everywhere, but it was clear he was not going to live. The bullet had severed most of the vessels in his head.

My husband and I looked at each other and then turned to the physician in charge.

"What's the purpose in taking him to another hospital?" my husband asked.

"He's still got a pulse and we have to do everything for him," the doctor responded.

And I thought, "The best thing to do for him would be to turn these machines off and let whatever happens, happen."

We had no choice, however, but to transport.

It took an hour to get him stabilized enough to move him. We got him on the ship, and he was so big, there was barely room for me to sit.

About five minutes after lift-off, he arrested on us. There was no room for me to do CPR, so I told my husband, "We'll just have to do this chemically, with drugs."

He was bleeding all over the place, basically

dead by now, but we did our procedures by rote, and at least got him to the hospital with a pulse.

In the emergency room, the team went into their trauma mode, and it was an exercise in futility all over again.

The whole thing was depressing and frustrating because it was a flight that never should have been. A waste of time. A waste of expense. And for what? What purpose did it serve?

Flights like these pose special problems for nurses and paramedics who may already feel insecure or uncertain about the tough decisions they are faced with daily regarding patient care.

Some flight personnel go into a perpetual state of self-doubt, constantly second-guessing themselves, wondering if their decisions will adversely affect a patient already near death. Many wind up discussing difficult cases with colleagues, who may or may not offer them support.

Others choose to go it alone, accepting the hard, cold fact that not every patient can be saved, or should be. . . .

You have to learn to put up a wall, because if you don't, you get yourself in trouble. People will crap out on you. You must accept it if you're going to stay in this business.

We picked up a lady involved in a car wreck, and when we got her ready to load, she was nodding and responding appropriately. Five minutes later, she went into respiratory failure, then cardiac arrest.

To watch someone die in front of you is very

unnerving, especially when you know you're doing everything you can. But it's something each one of us has to come to terms with sooner or later.

Things happen that we don't want to see. Things go wrong that we don't want to admit.

It's all part of what we do, and who we are.

# 10
## *Flight for Life*

*"This job lets you know how many ways you can get nailed, because we see the worst accidents and most critical patients. It can make you afraid to get up in the morning."*

—AirCare pilot

IT IS EARLY SUMMER ON A CLEAR FRIDAY MORNING in Winston-Salem, North Carolina, and Susan Butler, chief flight nurse for AirCare at North Carolina Baptist Hospital, is looking forward to the weekend. She has a trip planned and is anxious to leave the office. It is 7:00 A.M.—only twelve hours until the end of her shift.

Her crew, flight nurse Donna Eaton, thirty, and paramedic Jamie O'Neal, thirty-one, are organizing supplies. They are working today along with Captain Jim Aleshire, forty-seven, and thirty-eight-year-old co-pilot Guy Maher.

On the kitchen counter are a dozen glazed donuts, untouched. Donna eyes them surreptitiously, wondering if she'll skip lunch today. But her biggest problem isn't missing meals when she goes on a flight, it's holding her bladder, for there are no bathroom facilities in the aircraft.

# FLIGHT FOR LIFE

Outside the frame building that houses the program's office sits a $4.5 million Bell 412 helicopter, one of the largest aircraft in the air ambulance business. Its black exterior, with bright gold AIRCARE painted on its side, glistens in the morning sun. Because it transports only critically ill patients, it has been dubbed the "Deathstar." The crew doesn't seem to mind. They are used to dark humor.

Less than five hundred yards away is a stone-crafted memorial, simple and clean in design, built to honor the memory of a crew that perished in an Air-Care flight five years earlier.

Two flight nurses had relieved Susan and her partner that morning, or they would have been on the doomed flight that killed everyone on board. The close call was traumatic for Susan. Only after the memorial and dedication ceremony was she able to reconcile herself with the situation and go to work free of the anger and strong emotions that plagued her for weeks after the accident. The new quarters she and the crew just moved into have also helped her put the past behind and move on.

"Initially I felt a lot of anger toward the pilot involved in the accident," says Susan. "But I got past that phase. It helped getting out of our old quarters, because there were so many memories there. I could always visualize the team members we lost, see them in that facility, remembering our covered-dish suppers, getting our office organized, sitting through our certification exams. We had a lot of good times. I'll always miss them, as long as I'm involved in this business."

In a career that requires toughness, particularly

from its women, Susan Butler, at thirty-seven, looks more like a head cheerleader than a chief flight nurse. With her braided brown hair and dimpled smile, she is exuberant and pretty, the classic girl next door. Yet beneath that bright exterior exudes an air of competence. Patients instinctively trust her and, in a crisis, want her by their side.

She is responsible for the supervision of five full-time registered nurses, two part-time R.N.s, and four paramedics. All, including Susan, are hospital employees.

The flight team trusts her judgment and her management style. It's hands-off, allowing them to control their own responsibilities within their job descriptions.

Between 1986 and 1991, AirCare carried nearly three thousand patients from seventy-five referral hospitals, averaging two flights a day. About 15 percent of the transports were scene calls. Like all flight programs, AirCare operates around the clock, every day of the year.

But this morning has been calm so far. Pilot Jim Aleshire, an Illinois native with thirty years' flying experience, is comfortably ensconced on the couch in the lounge, watching TV. Tall and lean with a Jimmy Stewart smile, he has a calm demeanor that makes him a favorite among the crew—most of the time. Well known for his expertise in the cockpit, he has a way of making safe but sharp bank turns, the kind that send a stomach reeling. He is amused when Susan defends his unique style of flying.

"Get used to it," Susan tells her nurses and paramedics, "because some of us like it."

Copilot Guy Maher, originally from New Jersey,

sits nearby, scanning a business periodical. Off duty, he is a management consultant, and often refers to medical flights as the thing he likes to do most but for which he is paid the least. AirCare is one of only two medical flight programs in the country that routinely flies with both a pilot and copilot on board. Both Gary and Jim are employed by Air Methods, a company based in Denver, Colorado, that also leases AirCare helicopters and mechanics.

Guy is bored and tosses the magazine aside. For him, downtime—no flights, no calls—is the most stressful part of the job. It means he must literally wait for accidents to happen.

He looks at Jim.

"Hey, you remember that case . . . ?" he says, and they are off and running, swapping stories like baseball cards. It helps pass the morning.

The topic turns to unforgettable scene calls. Jim's version of a flight from hell is "anytime a nurse comes to work in a bad mood."

"Speaking of nurses," says Guy as Donna enters the room, "do you know the difference between a terrorist and Donna when she's in one of her moods? The difference is, you can negotiate with a terrorist."

"You dog," Donna responds in her thick southern drawl. A small-town North Carolinean, she is solidly built, with a pixie nose and the kind of mischievous eyes that crinkle when she smiles. Her pet peeve is the gawkers who gather at scene calls like so many birds of prey. It still astounds her to recall the time she witnessed a couple setting up lawn chairs near an accident.

She is mentor, cohort, and partner to paramedic

Jamie O'Neal. They could pass for brother and sister, even though he is a blond and she is a redhead. Both are pert and bubbly. During flights, en route to a patient, they have been known to break into a rousing rendition of "You've Lost That Lovin' Feeling." When a flight goes wrong or a patient goes bad, they quietly hold hands, each providing comfort for the other. Jamie says the busier he is, the better he likes it. As a result, when not flying, he is often found in the hospital's Emergency Department, enthusiastically assisting the nurses.

Now gathered into one room, the flight team is still recounting memorable on-the-job experiences. In that sense, they are no different from employees on any given job, comparing notes on their morning coffee break.

"Remember the time we went to pick up the patient who got bitten by a snake?" asks Donna. "They wanted us to bring the snake with us in the helicopter. And it wasn't dead! Can you imagine that?"

Guy remembers a public relations flight in which a group of Boy Scouts lined up outside the helicopter for autographs from the crew. Their most frequent question was how fast the bird could fly.

"We told each one a progressively quicker speed," he says. "That last kid thought we could go about five hundred miles per hour. We couldn't resist it."

Amid the laughter, a phone rings softly in the corner of the room.

"We've got a transport, guys," says Susan. "Looks like a bad one. Two patients fell into a cesspool at a sewage treatment plant that contained methane gas."

190

The mood, jovial only moments before, abruptly changes. To the crew, there is nothing bizarre or strange about people falling into cesspools. On the contrary, it is a call much like all others, a cry for help, the very reason they are here. Everyone springs into action, grabbing supplies, rushing toward the parked aircraft.

When airborne, Jim and Guy are instructed to land at an airport near the accident site. At this point, all the crew knows is that there are two patients and that the helicopter has no adequate landing zone at the plant.

A ground crew—paramedics and emergency technicians—have already arrived at the scene. Jamie, having done that work himself before joining AirCare, knows they are often the unsung heroes in emergency medicine. Their help in retrieving and stabilizing patients is critical in cases where the helicopter cannot properly land. Today their job was a dirty one, for it involved fishing both patients out of a fifty-foot tank containing highly explosive, toxic methane gas. Once the patients were out, everyone had to be hosed down before the AirCare team could even go near them. No one envied this scene call.

"What happened?" are Jamie and Donna's first words to the paramedics upon reaching the airport.

The ground crew explained that apparently the first patient, a thirty-ish white male, climbed over the top of the tank to repair a leaky valve, lost his footing, and fell headfirst into the murky water below. The second patient, an older man in his fifties, went after him. Before he could reach his coworker, however, he had a cardiac arrest. Both patients were now in critical condition.

Donna takes responsibility for the younger man, while Jamie handles the cardiac patient. This will be a "hot unload," meaning Jim and Guy will not turn off the engines once the helicopter touches the tarmac upon their return to Baptist Hospital. Getting the patients inside the emergency department as quickly as possible is the main priority.

"Baptist, this is AirCare, come in, please," says Donna over the radio. "I have a report on patient number one. Do you copy?"

"Go ahead," responds the emergency department physician. "We're standing by. Over."

"My patient becomes cyanotic at times. Right now he is intubated, but spontaneously breathing, and he looks like he's got some rib fractures on the left. Also, he has a possible head injury, with lacerations over the right eye. He is combative but restrained. We've got a sinus rhythm presently at a rate of about sixty to seventy. Pupils are sluggish to react. We do have a strong radial pulse on him. Can't obtain a blood pressure at this time due to his combativeness. We'd like to know if we can give him a sedation of some kind." Although flight nurses and paramedics are primarily responsible for their patients, all drug orders must be authorized by a physician.

"Is this the patient that fell?" the physician asks.

"Affirmative," says Donna. "Both patients fell about fifteen feet."

"Is either patient covered with sewage or is there any other need for decontamination?" asks the doctor.

"They were both decontaminated at the scene," replies Donna.

"Ten-four. Go ahead and administer two milligrams of Versed, IV."

Donna repeats the doctor's order. "Stand by for patient number two," she says.

"Okay, Doc," says Jamie, talking over the radio. "I have a patient, male, in his fifties, who we think went down to rescue the other patient but was overcome with methane gas. He's been decontaminated. When found, he was not able to be resuscitated until he was removed from the sewage. Moving caused him to take one breath. He is now intubated, but has no spontaneous respirations. Cardiac monitor shows sinus tachycardia [fast heartbeat] with a rate of one hundred twenty. Pupils now are two-three-plus and sluggish. He is unconscious, with a Glasgow score of three. He has two IVs, and we're hyperventilating him at twenty-eight to thirty-two breaths per minute."

"Did this patient suffer any trauma at the scene?" the doctor wants to know.

"No, sir, he did not."

Jim's voice interrupts the relay. From the cockpit, he updates Jamie on their estimated time of arrival at the hospital.

"We've got six to seven minutes till touchdown."

Back at AirCare headquarters, Susan Butler is monitoring the radio transmission.

"We'll need two oxygen tanks at the ramp," she says to herself. Her job now is to coordinate transfer of the patients from the helicopter to the hospital's emergency department. If necessary, she will also provide an extra pair of hands.

Outside, in the distance, she can hear the whirl of the blades as the helicopter approaches. The craft lightly touches down, and the doors spring open. Amid the tangle of stretchers, IV tubing, blankets, and monitoring equipment are the inert, pale forms of two very sick patients. Two hospital workers have been waiting, and are ready to help Donna, Jamie, and Susan unload the patients, whisking both men across the pavement to the open doors of the emergency department, where a medical team is prepared to treat their life-threatening injuries. In the end, after all their efforts, only one will survive; the older patient will not.

At the helicopter, Jim and Guy are winding down. There are a number of procedures to follow, including the refilling of oxygen tanks, refueling the aircraft, and the inevitable reports that must be written and filed after each flight. The interior of the craft must be cleaned out, and supplies restocked, to prepare the ship for other flight requests that may come in.

"So what do you think?" asks Guy as they head toward the office.

Jim shakes his head. "Doesn't look good," he says. "Bad scene."

Guy agrees, glancing over his shoulder toward the hospital's emergency department entrance. Beyond those double doors are two men not unlike themselves in many ways, who are fighting for their lives.

"I just hope," he says softly, "that this time we helped to make a difference."

# EPILOGUE

*"There are days filled with joy and elation, like when the patient shakes my hand before going home.*

*"And days that are empty and sad. Those are the times I know my face will be the last one seen, my voice the final one heard, before he dies.*

*"I worry that I'll grow callous to such things. Then I remind myself that my seeming lack of emotion is the only way to deal with these volatile extremes.*

*"Why do I continue putting on the flight suit, subjecting myself to what is, no doubt, a tragic environment?*

*"I think the answer is this: About the time I've had all the pain and suffering I can bear, someone comes up to me and says, 'You don't remember me, do you? I was your patient on so-and-so flight.'*

*"I always feel guilty when I don't recall the name or face.*

*"Then the conversation continues and my memory returns, including the part I never share—that I did not think he would survive. Yet here he is, alive and well.*

*Epilogue*

*"He walks away and I smile to myself, for something has changed. I feel rejuvenated.*

*"And I know that I am willing to tolerate the heartaches, just so I can be renewed one more time."*

> —Greg Lathrop,
> chief flight nurse
> MAMA crew
> Asheville, North Carolina

"Takes up where <u>SERPICO</u> and <u>PRINCE OF THE CITY</u> leave off."
—Darcy O'Brien, author of <u>Murder in Little Egypt</u>

# COP HUNTER

## The Shocking True Story of Corrupt Cops and the Man Who Went Undercover to Stop Them

## VINCENT MURANO
### With William Hoffer

Available from Pocket Books

POCKET
BOOKS

645

THE TRUE STORY OF A SUPER COP
AND HIS ONE-MAN WAR AGAINST CRIME!

# ONE TOUGH COP

## The Bo Dietl Story
### Bo Dietl and Ken Gross

*"Bo Dietl was probably the best detective in New York."*
—from the introduction by Nicholas Pileggi,
author of *Wiseguy*

*HE WENT AFTER NEW YORK'S
WORST CRIMINALS, WISEGUYS
AND PSYCHOPATHS—AND NEVER
USED HIS GUN!*

POCKET
B O O K S

Available from Pocket Books